AF148689

LOVE JIHAD
AND OTHER FICTIONS

LOVE JIHAD

AND OTHER FICTIONS

SIMPLE FACTS
TO COUNTER
VIRAL FALSEHOODS

SREENIVASAN JAIN
MARIYAM ALAVI
SUPRIYA SHARMA

ALEPH

ALEPH

ALEPH BOOK COMPANY
An independent publishing firm
promoted by *Rupa Publications India*

First published in India in 2024
by Aleph Book Company
7/16 Ansari Road, Daryaganj
New Delhi 110 002

Copyright © Sreenivasan Jain, Aruveetil Mariyam Alavi, and
Supriya Sharma 2024

All rights reserved.

The authors have asserted their moral rights.

The views and opinions expressed in this book are those
of the authors and the facts are as reported by them, which
have been verified to the extent possible, and the publishers
are not in any way liable for the same.

The publisher has used its best endeavours to ensure that
URLs for external websites referred to in this book are
correct and active at the time of going to press. However,
the publisher has no responsibility for the websites and can
make no guarantee that a site will remain live or that the
content is or will remain appropriate.

Cover illustration: Freepik

No part of this publication may be reproduced, transmitted,
or stored in a retrieval system, in any form or by any means,
without permission in writing from Aleph Book Company.

ISBN: 978-81-19635-59-7

1 3 5 7 9 10 8 6 4 2

Printed in India

This book is sold subject to the condition that it shall not,
by way of trade or otherwise, be lent, resold, hired out, or
otherwise circulated without the publisher's prior consent
in any form of binding or cover other than that in which it
is published.

Extraordinary claims require extraordinary evidence.

—Carl Sagan

CONTENTS

TODAY'S WHATSAPP FORWARD, TOMORROW'S LAW

Shah Rukh Khan is one of Bollywood's biggest stars. His movies are cultural touchstones, watched and rewatched across generations. At last count, he had 43 million followers on Twitter and nearly as many on Instagram. The adoration for him transcends boundaries, within and outside India.

But go by this Facebook post, and Khan is guilty of 'population jihad', supposedly a Muslim plot to overrun India's Hindu majority by producing more children.

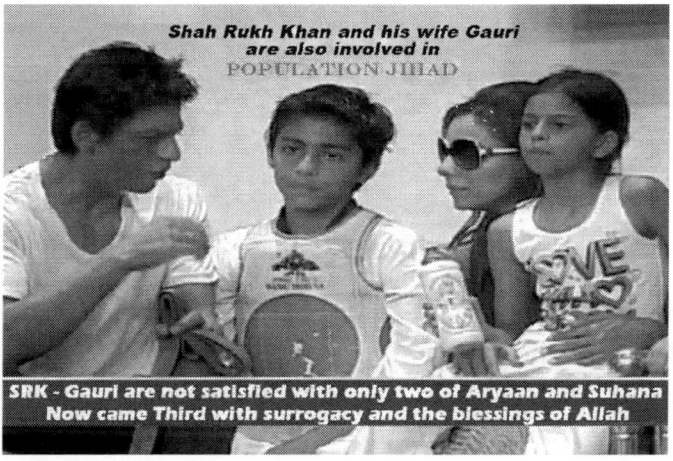

The evidence to back this implausible-sounding claim? None. Just the fact that Khan is the Muslim parent of three children is presented as proof of the thesis.

If this seems fantastical, consider this tweet.

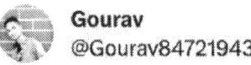

Gourav
@Gourav84721943   ...

Amir khan is the brand ambassador of love jihad..
First reena dutta and now kiran rao.
A true ' peaceful ' inspiration.
Respect to actors like akshay kumar and ajay devgan.
#Amirkhan #LoveJihad

Aamir Khan married a Hindu woman Reena Dutta in 1986, had 2 children "Junaid Khan" and "Ira Khan" and Got divorced in 2002.

Aamir Khan married another Hindu woman Kiran Rao in 2005, had a child "Azad Khan". Got divorced today in 2021.

5:14 PM · Jul 3, 2021

It accuses another Bollywood superstar, Aamir Khan, of being the 'brand ambassador of love jihad', a theory that claims Muslims are scheming to alter India's demography by seducing and converting Hindu women.

Again, the only evidence offered in support of this assertion are the religious identities of Khan and his former partners: while he is a Muslim man, they are Hindu women. Net result: 'love jihad'.

It isn't just the real lives of Bollywood stars that are grist to the WhatsApp mill. Even a fictional movie plot has been harnessed as evidence for yet another popular theory—Muslim appeasement, or the idea that Muslims are favoured over others.

शोले

शोले फिल्म में गांव में लाइट नहीं थी।

ठाकुर लालटेन लेकर घूमता था, लेकिन नमाज के टाइम लाउडस्पीकर बजता था।

क्योंकि राइटर जावेद अख्तर था और पिक्चर देखने वाले हम थे।

According to this WhatsApp forward, there was no electricity in the fictional village in which the blockbuster movie *Sholay* (1975) was set. And while a Hindu character (the Thakur) roamed around in the dark, the loudspeaker at the mosque came alive during the time of namaz. Why? Because the screenwriter of *Sholay* was Javed Akhtar, a Muslim.

◆

As journalists, we have spent a significant part of our professional lives examining the claims made by politicians, governments, and corporations: the conventional matrix of power.

In this book, however, we have chosen to turn our focus to a set of viral claims seemingly landing from nowhere in the WhatsApp chats and social media feeds of millions of Indians every day. Their proliferation signals a bizarre new normal, in which Shah Rukh Khan can be accused of 'population jihad' and Aamir Khan of 'love jihad', only because they are Muslim.

These conspiracy theories aren't new. They have lurked in the shadows of India's public square for decades. But they have now taken centre stage. Carried on the wings of social media, they operate in insidious ways. Unlike, say, an overblown government press release, which invites scepticism because it is seen as serving the interests of those in power, these conspiracy theories are often shared by people in our personal circles. The source could be a neighbour, a friend, a colleague, an ex-classmate or a relative, which creates the illusion of intimate endorsement. Courtesy this subterfuge, the narrative these theories push—of India's Hindu majority under threat from minorities—has seeped into the bones of our society, almost becoming the common sense of our times.

Yet for all their supposed 'organic' nature, the link between these viral theories and the formal apparatus of power is no secret. India is currently ruled by the Bharatiya Janata Party (BJP), which is part of a network of Hindutva organizations led by the Rashtriya Swayamsevak Sangh, and called the Sangh Parivar. Sharing its philosophy are scores of individuals and groups who advocate the idea that India is first and foremost a nation of Hindus, a fact that its religious minorities must accept. This book collectively calls them the Hindu Right.

'Population jihad' or 'love jihad' are constructs of the Hindu Right. Nowadays they are routinely platformed by high-ranking politicians, government functionaries, and wide swathes of the mainstream media. Some of these conspiracies have even been passed into law. Today's WhatsApp forward, astonishingly, can become tomorrow's legislation.

But what are the facts on which these constructs are based? What is the evidence to back them?

Is there something real here that we had missed all along?

We decided to bring hard-nosed journalistic scrutiny to Hindutva conspiracy theories, much in the way we would probe allegations of political corruption or corporate embezzlement. We filed Right to Information requests, looked up government records, searched through parliamentary questions, contacted leaders of the BJP and Sangh Parivar, read up academic research, and did on-the-ground reportage.

We realized early on, though, that investigating Hindutva conspiracy theories was like entering a hall of mirrors—how can you disprove a theory if you can't pin it down? This haziness partly stems from the fact that while many endorse these theories, no one claims ownership over them. Moreover, they are vaguely defined. For instance, the label of 'love jihad' can be applied to a seemingly infinite number of cases, making the task of fact-checking akin to a game of whack-a-mole— you manage to debunk one, and ten new ones show up. A new theory, or a sub-plot of an old theory, is born every day.

Given the impossibility of examining every single conspiracy theory, we picked the most enduring, commonly cited ones. (By the time the book is published, even these may have mutated.)

Chapter One takes on 'love jihad', perhaps the most ascendant of all the theories—there is even a movie on it, endorsed by the Prime Minister of India. But where did it all start? To find out, we probe what is held up as the Patient Zero case of 'love jihad'. We also investigate arguably the only definitive list of 'love jihad' cases. Through our RTI search, we zoom in on the Indian state that has made the largest number of arrests under the anti-'love jihad' law. We travel to the ground to explore: is the crackdown justified?

'Population jihad' is the rare theory where its proponents cite government data to back their astonishing claim—that Muslims are waging a holy war by producing more children and infiltrating India's borders. But does the data actually bear out the claim? In Chapter Two, we crunch the numbers and trawl through parliamentary records to decode whether Muslims will indeed outnumber over a billion Hindus in the near future.

It's not just Muslims who are in the crosshairs of viral theories. In Chapter Three, we scrutinize the Hindutva claim of a sinister Christian scheme to take over India through mass forced conversions. Is it true that Christian evangelists even managed to deceitfully convert the mother of a legislator in a southern Indian state? Was a student of a convent school forced to take her life because of the pressure to convert? Our ground investigation throws up answers.

Remember the far-fetched allegation related to *Sholay* at the beginning of this introduction, of Muslims being favoured when it comes to electricity supply? Chapter Four, which examines the claim of Muslim appeasement, begins with a real-world example of a strikingly similar accusation levelled by a top BJP leader—that a state run by a rival political party supplied more power on Eid as compared to Diwali. To fact-check the claim, we analyse decade-long electricity data. We also probe the long-standing tenets that prop up the charge of Muslim appeasement—hajj subsidy, funds to madrasas, and the favourite bugbear of the Hindu Right: Muslim men being able to take up to four wives.

So what's new, some readers may argue. These theories have been around for a long while. Why are we tackling them now? The short answer to this: because more than ever before, they now have the backing of power. A phenomenon we examine in the epilogue of this book, using data on the aftermath of India's 'pink revolution' moment, and the surge in VIP hate speech.

To make it easier to navigate the material, the structure of the book follows the fact-checking template. We have treated every conspiracy theory as a series of claims made by the Hindu Right. Each claim has been investigated separately, and we present a conclusion at the end of every section. We have included an exhaustive list of sources in the endnotes to the book.

We are writing this book in deeply polarized times. It is possible that some readers may perceive our focus to be selective or agenda driven. This is partly a reflection of the success of these conspiracy theories. Their flood is so relentless that even sensible Indians—who in our view constitute India's vast majority—have been primed to buy into them, and may see our questioning stance itself as a reflection of bias.

All we can say to that is: please read the book before you decide.

Sreenivasan Jain
Mariyam Alavi
Supriya Sharma

July 2023

Chapter 1

'LOVE JIHAD'

On a humid afternoon in August 2014, in a modest house on the edges of the bustling city of Meerut in western Uttar Pradesh, we sat across from a young woman, her face heavily masked with a dupatta. We were there to interview her because an appalling ordeal she had described to the police was reverberating far beyond the borders of Meerut.

In July, she had gone missing from home. Two weeks later, she resurfaced with a surgery scar on her stomach and a certificate of her conversion from Hinduism to Islam. Her explanation, filed as a police complaint by her family, was horrifying: she said she had been abducted by a group of Muslim men from her village, taken to a madrasa in the nearby town of Hapur, gang-raped, and forcibly converted to Islam. Her captors included Nawab, the village pradhan, and Sanaullah, a local cleric. She had been impregnated during the rape and put through an abortion, resulting in the abdominal scar.

The brutality, coupled with the religious dimension, invoked the spectre of 'love jihad', the contested theory of a conspiracy by Muslim men to seduce and convert Hindu women, with a view to overrun India's Hindus.

Largely confined to the shadows of public conversation, the sensational theory was rapidly gaining traction in regions like western Uttar Pradesh where Hindus and Muslims live in close, sometimes volatile, proximity and where interreligious relationships often contribute to the tensions. Local leaders of the Sangh Parivar and the BJP had descended on Meerut to amplify the young woman's account. The media coverage was, for the most part, lurid. Meerut was on the edge.

It was in this fraught mix that we had come to report the story. The challenges were considerable. Paramount in cases of alleged sexual violence is the need to respect the testimony of the survivor. This is all the more necessary in states like Uttar Pradesh, where the embedded conservatism of the social order—and the criminal justice system—makes the path to justice deeply challenging for women battling sexual violence.

Yet, the framing of the Meerut episode by the Hindu Right as an Islamic conspiracy warranted greater scrutiny. Just eleven months ago, riots had broken out in the neighbouring district of Muzaffarnagar, in which more than sixty people had been killed. The trigger was widely believed to have been a 'love jihad' rumour, for which we had found no credible evidence in our reporting.

In the Meerut case, the police arrested close to a dozen Muslim men. As the investigation progressed, however, they found multiple inconsistencies in the statement of the young woman, from mix-ups over the date and location of the sexual assault to conflicting versions of the names of the alleged rapists.

Given the widespread publicity around the episode, the woman's family allowed journalists to seek clarifications from her directly—unusual in rape investigations. That is how we met her in her house, her identity concealed. When we asked her about the conflicting versions, she blamed the police. 'What can I do if they made mistakes while noting down my statements?' she said.

At the home of Nawab, the elected village chief, a different story emerged. His relatives and neighbours told us the young woman had been coached by Nawab's Hindu rivals, who were smarting over an election defeat. 'After thirty-five years, a Muslim became the pradhan. The Hindus were upset about that,' said Nazakat Ali, Nawab's neighbour. The relatives claimed Nawab had an alibi for the dates when he had supposedly abducted her.

They also said the young woman had friendly ties to the Muslim community, courtesy her stint as an English teacher in the local madrasa. This was confirmed by Mohammed Ameeruddin, the administrator of the school.

At the government hospital where the young woman had been admitted, Shakun Singh, the doctor who attended to her, told us the procedure she underwent was not an abortion, as stated in her police complaint, but a surgery for a ruptured ectopic pregnancy. In an ectopic pregnancy, the foetus develops outside the uterus. Experts said it takes over a month to detect such pregnancies, raising questions over the young woman's claim of being impregnated and requiring an abortion within the two weeks she had gone missing.

The doctor at the Meerut hospital said the woman had come with a few companions, one of whom, a young man named Kaleem, had signed as 'husband' in the medical form for her surgery. The police had arrested Kaleem on the basis of the signature, but curiously the young woman had not mentioned him in any of her accounts. As we conducted more interviews in the village, Kaleem's name came up repeatedly as a pivotal figure in the entire case. The implication, denied by both the woman and Kaleem's family, was of a secret relationship between the two of them, during the course of which she likely developed a pregnancy complication.

A representative of an Uttar Pradesh-based group that works with embattled Hindu–Muslim couples told us the Meerut episode, while deeply worrisome, was not unusual. 'When adult men and women get into relationships that families do not approve of, all hell breaks loose and criminal cases are filed against the boy,' said Seema Misra of the Association for Advocacy and Legal Initiatives Trust. 'There is immense pressure on the girl to say she was taken against her will. Nowadays, it is given a communal colour for political gain.'

Cut to a year and a half later. On 6 December 2015, in the inside pages of *The Hindu*, a photograph appeared of a coy bride and a somewhat stiff looking groom, captioned 'Kaleem, with his bride Shalu Tyagi'.

A photograph of the Meerut couple appeared in The Hindu
on 6 December 2015.

In that one image, and the accompanying headline— 'For Meerut's "love jihad" couple, 3-year courtship ends in "nikah"'—the entire edifice of the Meerut case collapsed.

Almost like a movie unspooling in reverse, *The Hindu* story recounted how the young woman, Shalu (who could now be named since she was not, by her own account, a rape survivor) escaped her family home in October 2014, and approached the police to submit a written statement withdrawing her charge of gang rape and abduction. Shalu told the police that she was forced to file the rape complaint by her father. 'I went with the boy belonging to a different community out of my own will,' she said in her statement.

Shalu added that a local BJP leader, Vineet Agarwal, had paid her family ₹25,000 just a few days after the case came to light and offered to pay more if they would stick to their charges of gang rape. Agarwal, quoted in the *Times of India,* accepted he had paid money to the family, but said that it was only because they were financially weak.

Kaleem had been granted bail in April 2015, paving the way for the couple to marry. *The Hindu* report said the wedding ceremony was attended by Kaleem's parents. Shalu's parents stayed away.

◆

For all of India's vibrant social diversity, interfaith relationships are a rarity.

Only 2.6 per cent of marriages in India are interreligious, according to the National Family Health Survey data, from 2015-16. (In the absence of an official count of interfaith marriages, this survey data serves as the closest approximation.)

In the feverish imagination of Hindutva groups, however, relationships between Hindu women and Muslim men are neither rare, nor benign—they are part of a vast and sinister Muslim conspiracy that poses no less than an existential threat to India.

'Save India from love jihad', says the cover story in the 16-20 September 2020 edition of Hindu Vishva, *the in-house magazine of the Vishva Hindu Parishad.*

This panic isn't new. A century ago, in the 1920s, Hindu organizations had drummed up a campaign on 'Hindu aauraton ki loot', or the loot of Hindu women, with even a riot erupting in the town of Mathura in Uttar Pradesh after a Muslim man eloped with a Hindu woman.

But only in recent years has this panic resurfaced and coalesced into a nationwide theory that goes under a catchy term—'love jihad'. Even the collapse of high-profile cases like the Meerut episode has done little to impede its spread.

Interfaith couples are now routinely harassed, even beaten up. The violence is endorsed by high-ranking politicians who threaten 'love jihad' conspirators with reprisals. Hindutva groups continue to rally crowds and stoke anger on the issue. By one count, in Maharashtra alone, in a span of four months, fifty public marches were taken out against 'love jihad' (and other forms of 'jihad').

The term 'love jihad' is not defined under the law, the Ministry of Home Affairs said in response to a parliamentary query in 2020. Yet, several Indian states have passed what are known as anti-'love jihad' laws.

What is the evidence propping up the theory?

In this chapter, we try to find out, starting with a search for the origins of the term.

◆

CLAIM: 'Love jihad' is real because...Christians in Kerala first raised it

In the summer of 2022, we contacted several Hindutva organizations that propagate the 'love jihad' theory and sought interviews with them on the subject. Alok Kumar, spokesperson of the Vishva Hindu Parishad (VHP), met us in his Delhi office.

'The word 'love jihad' was first used by the Christians in Kerala,' Kumar told us.

This is a common claim pushed by proponents of 'love jihad', possibly as validation that the theory is not an Islamophobic fantasy conjured up by Hindi-belt Hindutvavadis.

The facts are a bit unclear. Some reports claim the Hindu

Janajagruti Samiti, a Hindutva organization, first began to use the term in Karnataka in 2007. Others point out that at the Catholic Bishops Council in Kerala in 2009, a bishop reportedly warned the gathering—without evidence—that Muslims were luring away Catholic girls.

What is more certain is that the term made its first official appearance in the proceedings of the Kerala High Court.

On 7 August 2009, two men petitioned the court, seeking its help with finding their daughters who had slipped out of their homes in the early hours of 18 July. The men feared their daughters had been entrapped by a senior student who wanted to convert them to his religion in the garb of marriage.

The daughters were not minors. Both Mithula Madhavan and Bino Jacob were twenty-three-year-old students pursuing a master's in Business Administration from a college in Pathanamthitta district.

Mithula was Hindu. Bino was Christian. The senior student, Shahan Sha, was Muslim.

On 12 August, Justices R. Basant and M. C. Hari Rani of the Kerala High Court directed the police to form a Special Investigative Team to look for the women.

Nine days later, the women appeared in court—with their husbands. Mithula was now married to Shahan Sha; Bino to Shahan Sha's friend, Sirajudeen. The women told the judges that they were in love with the men and had married them 'voluntarily and willingly'. The judges recorded that the women 'were reluctant to even speak to their parents'. But they persuaded them to go back with their parents: 'it is only with much persuasion exercised by us in the interest of harmony that they agreed to speak to their parents and go with them', they noted.

Among the conditions laid down by the judges was that the parents would allow the women to speak with their husbands on the phone and would bring them back to the court on 28 August.

On 24 August, however, the young men rushed back to the court, complaining that they had been denied access to their wives. The court summoned the women. When they showed up on 26 August, they took a completely different stand—they said they 'do not want to have anything to do' with their husbands.

Justices Basant and Hari Rani recorded in their order: 'The reasons that prompt the alleged detenues to change their stand now…is of course a little confusing, but the fact remains that we have to respect the wishes and desire of the alleged detenues who have crossed the age of 22 years.'

The judges had felt no such need earlier, when they had sent them home with their parents, against their wishes.

Fourteen years later, Shahan Sha still remembers the shock he felt when he saw Mithula's face in court that day. 'She looked drugged, her eyes were red,' he told us, when we met him in a public park in Kochi on an overcast day in July 2023.

Now a manager in an e-commerce company, Shahan Sha lives a quiet life with his wife and children. He was initially reluctant to speak to us, but then ended up recounting the tumultuous events that had led to that day in 2009—an account that also features in a petition he filed in the court.

Shahan Sha was born and raised in Pathanamthitta, a town in central Kerala. His family was locally prominent. His grandfather was a district leader of the Indian Union Muslim League (IUML), an ally of the Congress. Shahan Sha himself was the district president of the Muslim Students Federation, the student wing of IUML. After completing a bachelor's degree in biotechnology, he joined the MBA programme in a local college, which, despite its small size, had attracted students from across Kerala. 'Many of them would come home,' Shahan Sha recalled. 'My mother would cook biryani for them.' Among those were Mithula and her friend Bino.

The first time he had struck up a conversation with Mithula, he recalled, was when he had spotted her crying in the college library. The exchange gradually led to a friendship. In an email sent in March 2008, which is part of the court record, addressing him with a term of endearment 'Shachettan', Mithula wrote: 'I was born into a lot of problems... No one in my family even remembers my birthday... When you know my problems, Shachettan's mind will also be pained... For every problem u r my instant cure friend.'

Shahan Sha said he began to care for the troubled, soft-spoken woman. Love blossomed. In an email in May 2008, she wrote, 'Didn't Shachettan tell me once that you are scared of loving anyone? I also had the same fear till I met Shachettan. But I never felt that fear with Shachettan. That is why I loved so much and became close.'

Shahan Sha said he was anxious about the prospect of interfaith love, but Mithula was firm. 'You should forgo any plans to abandon me. Everyone may lose me. And you should not be the reason for that,' she wrote in the email, signing off with: 'May ALLAH b wit u...'

By this time, both Mithula and Bino had started studying Islam, Shahan Sha said. They were curious about religion, he claimed. When they came to his home, they borrowed books on Islam. Worried by their growing interest in Islam—and their closeness to Shahan Sha—the women's parents took them out of college.

But they managed to stay in touch with Shahan Sha, texting him frequently on the phone. In July 2009, the messages and calls acquired a sense of urgency: Bino said her parents wanted to take her abroad, Mithula said her parents were planning to marry her off. They wanted to leave home and go to Ponnani, a centre for Islamic learning. Shahan Sha said he decided to help them escape.

But within days, the group realized that the police were looking for them. Shahan Sha recalled that his family was interrogated. They met a lawyer who advised them to get married—the court will send unmarried women back to their parents, he said. Shahan Sha's friend, Sirajudeen, offered to marry Bino; she accepted his proposal. On 12 August, the women converted to Islam and married the men in a religious ceremony.

Marriage eventually did not protect the young women. A two-judge bench sent them back to their parents. Facing criminal charges and fearing arrest, Shahan Sha and Sirajudeen filed bail applications. These came up before another judge, Justice K. T. Sankaran, on 29 September. To their great shock, Justice Sankaran accepted the police's version of events. More consequentially, he saw a larger conspiracy at play.

'It is stated that there is a movement or project which is called 'Romeo Jihad' or 'Love Jihad' conceived by a section of the Muslims,' he said. 'It is stated that Muslim boys are directed to pretend love to girls of other religions and get them converted to Islam. Lot of money is available for executing the project. There are men whose help is available at any time. Organisations are also there to implement the project.'

The order did not specify the source of these assertions.

Justice Sankaran directed the Director General of Police (DGP) in Kerala to respond, within three weeks, to eight questions, starting with whether a 'love jihad' movement existed within the state. He also sought replies from the central government.

On 18 October, Kerala's DGP, Jacob Punnoose, reported back to Justice Sankaran to say 'No organization or movement called 'Love Jihad' or 'Romeo Jihad' is so far identified as working in Kerala'. Yet, he added that 'there are reasons to suspect that there are concerted attempts to persuade girls to change their religion after they fall in love with Muslim boys.'

Finding the DGP's responses 'vague', Justice Sankaran asked him to produce in a sealed cover all the reports he had received from district units of the police.

The DGP reiterated in November 2009 that 'no concrete and sustainable evidence was available to establish that an organised movement called 'Love Jihad' was operating in the State of Kerala'. He ascribed his previous contradictory responses to 'the divergence which existed in the contents of reports received from different subordinate units'. While fifteen of the eighteen reports said there was no evidence for 'love jihad', based on 'source inputs', three reports 'suggested the clandestine designs of certain groups aimed at religious conversion through deceitful means, inter alia, under the guise of love'. The DGP clarified that 'source reports are often based on hearsay. They are usually not supported by any direct evidence.'

Overlooking the broad thrust of the police findings, on 9 December, Justice Sankaran passed an order suggesting that the Kerala government consider enacting a law, as some states have done, to prohibit forcible or deceitful conversion. He also rejected Shahan Sha and Sirajudeen's withdrawal petitions, and dismissed their bail applications.

This would have ordinarily paved the way for the men's arrest. But fortuitously, just a week ago, on 2 December, a petition they had filed seeking the striking down of charges against them had come up before another judge, Justice M. Sasidharan Nambiar. It led to a stay on their arrest.

The fresh petition had been drafted by lawyer P. K. Ibrahim, who had initially followed the case from afar, through sensational news coverage about Shahan Sha being a 'Lashkar terrorist' who was part of an Islamic conspiracy of 'love jihad'. He told us he had felt a growing sense of alarm. 'The entire community was in the dock,' he said. When Shahan Sha came to meet him and showed him Mithula's emails and messages, he asked: 'Why hasn't this material been made public?'

Ibrahim then proceeded to ensure the material came on the record. In the petition he filed, he included Mithula's correspondence with Shahan Sha, as well as an email that Mithula's brother had written to her after she had eloped. 'If you had at least indicated to me about your intentions then I would have talked to the parents and find a solution,' the brother wrote in the email dated 13 August. 'I know you was looking for a freedom from parents as you doesn't like to get married from our caste and religion (sic).'

Ibrahim also made Shahan Sha and Sirajudeen shoot off letters to the chief minister, the chief secretary, and the home department, highlighting that the police investigation itself was biased since top police officers were related to Mithula and Bino's families—this was also mentioned in the petition.

After going through the petition, Justice Nambiar asked for the case diary—the police's record of the case. When he saw the case diary on 17 December, he did not mince any words: 'Conduct of the Investigating Officer shocks the judicial conscience,' he noted.

As he pointed out, while recording the statements of the women, the police had not only taken their signatures—prohibited under the criminal procedure code—but also their thumb impressions.

'Both the so-called victims were postgraduates,' Justice Nambiar recalled when we met him in July 2023 at his Kochi residence where he now lives a retired life. 'If a witness is able to sign, there is no need for a thumb impression,' he said. The fact that the police had gone to the extent of taking thumb impressions suggested they wanted the women to feel that 'they can't retract' their statements later, he explained.

Justice Nambiar's scrutiny of the police record set off a sequence of events that culminated in the police withdrawing the cases against Shahan Sha and Sirajudeen. They did so by submitting 'refer reports', filed when cases are found to be false or based on mistaken facts.

India's original 'love jihad' case had collapsed. But this time, there were no screaming stories in the media.

In December 2010, taking note of the police withdrawal, Justice Nambiar wrote a short, perfunctory order: 'Petitions are dismissed as infructuous.'

Retired judges rarely speak to journalists. But perhaps there is a reason why Justice Nambiar spoke to us: 'I regret not writing a judgment in the case,' he said.

Compared to orders, which are typically short, a judgment is a lengthy exposition by a judge on the reasons for arriving at a particular view. Judgments are later cited as precedents in other cases.

Justice Sankaran's judgment, running into thirty-two pages, continues to be frequently cited, both inside and outside courtrooms, as evidence that the Kerala High Court had found merit in the 'love jihad' theory. This, even though the case that formed the basis of the judgement no longer stands. 'Ideally, after the case collapsed, Justice Sankaran should have recalled the judgment,' said Ibrahim, the lawyer.

But that did not happen. 'There is no other judgment on the record, except what was written by Justice Sankaran,' Justice Nambiar rued.

When asked what he would have written had he penned down a judgment, Justice Nambiar said: 'Marrying someone from another faith is not an offence. What is freedom if you can't eat what you want, if you can't marry whom you want.'

Shahan Sha eventually ended his marriage with Mithula.

He still thinks about her, though. 'I want to meet Mithula once before I die,' he told us. 'I want to ask her what wrong did I commit.'

CONCLUSION: No clear evidence of conspiracy was found in the original first cases of 'love jihad' in Kerala.

◆

CLAIM: 'Love jihad' is real because...it's everywhere

The origin story of 'love jihad' stands debunked. Bring this up with proponents of the theory and they pivot. They begin to reel off anecdotal examples with seemingly no connection to show 'love jihad' is a continuing menace. How does one fact-check a data set this undefined?

As a starting point, we zeroed in on three recent landmark cases cited as proof of 'love jihad'.

THE HADIYA CASE, KERALA, 2016

Seven years after Kerala's 'love jihad' bogey reached a dead end, a major controversy erupted in the state after a twenty-three-year-old Hindu woman named Akhila converted to Islam, became Hadiya, and married a Muslim man.

Her father moved the Kerala High Court, claiming she had been abducted and hoodwinked into conversion. He didn't just stop there: he alleged Hadiya was going to be transported out of the country to Syria. Hindutva groups saw the hand of the Popular Front of India (PFI), an Islamic organization that was later banned by the central government for terrorist activities. They claimed PFI had organized a groom for her from amongst their members.

According to media reports, Hadiya's fascination with Islam

was sparked not by the PFI, but by observing the prayer rituals of her Muslim friends from college. Eventually, when she decided to convert to Islam, Aboobacker, the father of her college friends, took her to an organization that issued conversion certificates. But to get a certificate, she needed to clear a religious exam. To prepare for the exam, Hadiya took a course offered by Sathya Sarini, an Islamic centre supported by PFI.

Hadiya did not convert for marriage—the conventional definition of 'love jihad'. She met and married her husband, Shefin Jahan, a former member of the PFI's student wing, almost a year after her conversion to Islam.

Hadiya and her husband told the court their marriage was consensual. But the high court annulled their marriage and sent Hadiya to her parents' custody. The matter went to the Supreme Court, which ordered India's federal anti-terrorism organization, the National Investigation Agency (NIA), to probe Hadiya's case, as well as conduct a wider inquiry into a possible conspiracy behind interfaith marriages and religious conversions in Kerala.

In March 2018, the Supreme Court restored Hadiya's marriage, saying, 'The strength of our Constitution lies in its acceptance of the plurality and diversity of our culture. Intimacies of marriage, including the choices which individuals make on whether or not to marry and on whom to marry, lie outside the control of the state.'

It allowed the NIA to continue its wider inquiry. In October 2018, the media reported that the NIA's probe had not unearthed any proof of conspiracy.

KASHMIR'S 'LOVE JIHAD' OUTBREAK, 2021

In the summer of 2021, reports surfaced of a 'love jihad' outbreak in another region—Jammu and Kashmir. Adding a sensational twist to the story were claims that Muslim men were not targeting Hindus, but women from Kashmir's tiny Sikh community.

The trigger was the case of Manmeet Kaur, nineteen, who became Zoya before marrying a Muslim man. Her family filed a case against her husband, Shahid Bhat, who was arrested on charges of abduction and forced conversion. Soon, social media was awash with posts about the spread of 'love jihad' in Kashmir. In some, Bhat was cast as a fifty-five-year-old man preying on a young Sikh woman. Bhat was, in fact, twenty-nine at the time of the wedding.

A social media post on 'love jihad' in Kashmir.

Two earlier instances of Kashmir-based Sikh women who had married Muslims were clubbed with Zoya's case to bolster the claim of a 'love jihad' outbreak: that of Danmeet Kaur, twenty-eight, and Viron Pal Kaur, renamed Khadeeja. Amongst those stoking the claims was the Akali Dal politician Manjinder Singh

Sirsa, who later joined the BJP. In a series of tweets, Sirsa urged the union home minister to bring a law in Jammu and Kashmir 'just like Uttar Pradesh and Madhya Pradesh'. Both states, as we shall see later, have passed so-called anti-'love jihad' laws.

All three women asserted in and outside court that they had made choices of their own will.

'So what if I am young? No one forced me,' Zoya can be heard responding, in a viral video clip, to a woman who is repeatedly trying to convince her to come back to her family.

But Zoya's protestations did not matter. The family and community took over. She was married off to a Sikh man within weeks. Sirsa, the politician, posted a celebratory tweet shortly afterwards, referring to her by her Sikh name—Manmeet Kaur.

A tweet posted by a Sikh politician Manjinder Singh Sirsa, about bringing back a woman from the community who had married a Muslim man.

In another undated viral video, Danmeet can be seen rubbishing allegations of 'love jihad', saying she had married her batchmate, Muzaffar, out of choice. She did face a threat, she said—not from Muslim conspiracists but from her own community. 'I was warned that I would get killed or targeted in acid attacks,' she said.

Khadeeja moved the high court for protection for herself and her husband, citing threats from the Sikh community. In a video, she said, 'There is no question of "love jihad" at gunpoint. I want to appeal to you all, please for God's sake don't make this a political issue. There is an attempt to break the brotherhood in Kashmir…of the Muslim and Sikh communities.'

AAFTAB-SHRADDHA, DELHI, 2022

In the final months of 2022, a gruesome murder case made front page headlines across India. Its basic outline is widely known: Aaftab Poonawalla, twenty-eight, was a food blogger. Shraddha Walkar, twenty-seven, worked for a call centre in Mumbai. They met on a dating app, first living together in Mumbai before shifting to Delhi in May 2022. According to the police, within days of the move, Aaftab killed Shraddha over an argument, chopped her body into thirty-five pieces and dumped them in different locations across Delhi.

In Hindutva circles, the horrific crime rapidly metamorphosed into 'love jihad'. Social media was aflame.

हिंदू राष्ट्र हिंदुत्व की पहचान
14 November 2022 · 🌐

Shraddha and Aftab zamin's so called love story!!

A girl named Shraddha eloped with Aftab Zamin and they started staying in live in relationship.

When Shraddha started to ask him to get married, he cut her into 35 pieces and stuffed her body parts in a fridge.

For the past few months, he had been taking out one piece a day to dispose off the body.

Finally he has been caught!!

Ladies, choose your partner wisely !! You never know which cute face is a predator.

Still, mera abdullah alag hai gang will never realise!! 🐑

#Love #jihad
👇👇👇👇👇👇👇👇
https://youtu.be/jS3Gf4_bDl8

❤️😮 392   39 💬 103 ↪

A social media post linked the Shraddha Walkar murder case to 'love jihad'.

Politicians amplified the conspiracy angle from public platforms. The chief minister of Assam, Himanta Biswa Sarma, at a BJP election event in Gujarat, said: 'There are many other stories like that of Aaftab and Shraddha in India. The country needs strict laws against 'love jihad'.'

Aside from their religious identities—Aaftab is Muslim, Shraddha was Hindu—there was no proof of any conspiracy. Shraddha had not converted to Islam. According to the police, there was no evidence of a religious dimension to the crime.

More bewilderingly, the 'love jihad' tag had been slapped on to a murder case. Remember, the conventional understanding of 'love jihad' is that it's a Muslim plot to seduce and convert Hindu women. In this definition, the goal is to amass new recruits to Islam by making the proposition attractive enough for Hindu women to give up their faith. How does *killing* Hindu women meet that aim?

In the Hindu Right ecosystem, this definitional sleight of hand is commonplace. The 'love jihad' label is routinely used for gender crimes where the male partner is Muslim and the woman is Hindu.

To be clear, gender violence in India is a pervasive menace. In the past decade, rapes have gone up by 27.10 per cent. Kidnapping of women has risen by 96.98 per cent. The latest round of the National Family Health Survey, conducted in 2019-20, shows almost 30 per cent of married women aged 18–49 have faced spousal violence—physical or sexual.

But to give gender violence a sectarian hue, as the 'love jihad' ecosystem seeks to do, is divisive and fallacious.

The fallacy fell apart quickly. In the months following the Shraddha case, the media reported brutal killings of women by their male partners, similar to the 'Aaftab-Shraddha' modus operandi, with one difference—both the accused and victim were Hindus. For instance, in February 2023, Delhi-based Sahil Gehlot was accused of strangling his live-in partner Nikki Yadav and storing her body in a fridge in a roadside dhaba in Najafgarh, Delhi. In the same month, Mumbai-based Hardik Shah was charged with killing his live-in partner Megha Torvi and stuffing her body in a storage space under the bed.

Did any of these murders agitate the Hindu Right? No prizes for guessing.

CONCLUSION: None of the landmark cases of 'love jihad' amount to proof of a Muslim conspiracy. Rather, they are consensual interfaith relationships. Or, as in the case of Aaftaab-Shraddha, intimate partner violence given a communal spin.

◆

CLAIM: 'Love jihad' is real because...the VHP has compiled a list of cases

High-profile cases talked up as 'love jihad' don't add up. But what if there are lesser-known cases that have escaped public attention?

To find out, we contacted four social media accounts almost entirely devoted to pushing the 'love jihad' narrative. This included the Facebook page 'Girls - Beware of Love Jihad', with 27,000 followers; 'India Against Love Jihad' with 7500 followers; 'Hindu against love jihad', with 4,100 followers; and 'Protest Love Jihad', with over 4,000 followers.

Two accounts replied. The somewhat garbled response from 'Hindu against love jihad' is reproduced verbatim.

> Miss alwavi you don't want to learn about this love johad rapidly growing in hindu community with one particular target to destroy hindusm.In fact a muslm girl want to or a boy a want to married with same girl then community destroyed him or his family

The response from 'Protest Love Jihad' was equally strange.

> All Posts on Our Page is neither a Claim or Misleading story
> Every post is associated with proper evidence published in media either print or electronic.

Additionally, we contacted mainstream Hindutva organizations that promote the 'love jihad' theory, such as the RSS and the VHP.

We asked the VHP's Kumar if he could define 'love jihad'.

'I don't know if there is a very precise definition,' Kumar admitted, with a laugh.

'I do not dispute that two adult persons have the right to marry as they like. But there are cases where the consent of the girl is obtained by deception,' he said. 'A deception includes the concealment of religion by the boy, wearing

Hindu things like the tilak or the kalawa (thread tied around the wrist), conveying that he is a Hindu, befriending the Hindu girl and marrying her. That may be what is broadly called "love jihad".'

A post from one of the pages devoted to pushing the 'love jihad' narrative.

In September 2020, while launching a special edition of the VHP's in-house magazine, entirely devoted to 'love jihad', Kumar had described this strategy as 'demographic invasion' by Muslims to reduce Hindus to a minority. We asked him: Does he have proof of this conspiracy? Numbers to back up the claim?

Kumar said he didn't have any numbers off the top of his head, but pointed us to the special edition, which featured a list of 'love jihad' cases.

The magazine, which we received in PDF form, was laced with deeply Islamophobic imagery and language.

Regardless, as the only comprehensive documentation of the 'love jihad' phenomenon collated by a recognized organization, we examined it in detail.

Very quickly, it became clear that the VHP had not carried out any independent investigation. Their list was simply a catalogue of 147 media reports—quite likely the outcome of a Google search. The earliest entry was from November 2011 and the last from September 2020, the date of the magazine's publication.

On closer analysis, seventy-three or almost half of all entries were invalid. They were either dead links, repetitions, instances not related to India, links to statements by politicians and public figures, commentary pieces on 'love jihad', or articles that carried their own lists of so-called 'love jihad' cases. The list also skipped serial numbers—for example, jumping from entry 8 to entry 10.

That left us with seventy-four unique cases in a span of nine years. Looking through them, we found that the 'love jihad' tag had been applied to a wide spectrum of gender-related crimes, across twenty-five categories: fraud, blackmail, abduction, abandonment, intimidation, dowry demands, rape, murder, and so on. The only common feature in these cases was that the accused was a Muslim man, the alleged victim a Hindu woman. As we had explained before, it is illogical to argue that such crimes are part of a 'love jihad' conspiracy, if the aim is to seduce and convert Hindu women.

In only two categories did religious identity have a role to play: Muslims hiding their name to dupe Hindu women into marrying them (Kumar's definition of 'love jihad'), and instances of forcible conversion to Islam.

कंपनियाँ बनाती हैं, जिसमें सर्वधर्म के नाम पर हिन्दू लड़कियों के मन में मुसलिम लड़कों के प्रति सहानुभूति भरी जा सके।

भारत का फिल्म व्यवसाय लगभग 9 दशकों से जारी है। दिलीप कुमार से सहानुभूति का भूत सिर पर चढ़ा, जो अब तक बरकरार है। दिलीप कुमार का असली नाम युसुफ खान हुआ करता था।

ऐसे कई लोग हैं, जो अपना नाम बदलकर अपने हित साधने में लगे हैं। फिल्मी दुनियाँ के खेल में ही कंपनी ही नहीं, बल्कि पूरी साजिश के तहत जिहादियों ने हर कदम पर कहानी और अभिनेताओं को बदला। कहानी लिखने वाले हो या गाना लिखने वाला, इन सब पर प्रभाव जिहादियों का रहा। राम तेरी गंगा मैली फिल्म में गंगा को उस जगह पर सुरक्षित दिखाया जाता है, जिनके मौलानाओं के बारे में आए दिन समाचार पत्रों में बच्चियों के साथ यौन शोषण की खबरें छपती रहती है। जबकि मंदिर में उस पर खतरा दिखाया जाता है, जिसके बारे में अब तक एक भी संदिग्ध बात सुनने या देखने को नहीं मिली है।

आवाज के मामले में जिहाद नहीं चल पाया, क्योंकि जो दर्शक को पसंद होता है, वही हिट होता है। ऐसे में गाना सुनने के बजाय गाना देखने के संस्कार पैदा किये गए। 20 के दशक से ही हिन्दू हिरोइन और मुस्लिम किरदार के एक नए युग का सूत्रपात हो गया था। उर्दू को एक धर्मनिरपेक्ष भाषा बनाकर लोगों के बीच परोसी जा रही थी और कहा जा रहा था कि भाषा वो होती है, जो आम लोग आसानी से समझ सकें। फिल्म जगत का हाल देखने से पता चल जाता है कि मुस्लिम हीरो के घर हिन्दू लड़कियाँ गईं। हालांकि प्यार का दंभ भरने वाली इन हिरोइनों को वहाँ कोई अच्छी जिन्दगी नहीं मिली, यह बात जग जाहिर है। फिल्मी दुनियाँ पर जिहादियों की पकड़ मजबूत होती गई। तो कुछ अभिनेताओं को छोड़ ज्यादातर हिन्दू अभिनेता दूसरी पंक्ति में खड़े हो गए। इस दौर में एक विशेष बात देखने को मिली कि पहले जो मुस्लिम अभिनेता हिन्दू नाम से ख्याति पा रहे थे, अब वैसा नहीं रहा। मुस्लिम अभिनेता पहली पंक्ति

में खड़े हो गए और उनके नाम भी मुसलमानों वाले ही रहे। अर्थात् जिहादियों की पहली साजिश सफल रही। मुस्लिम अभिनेता और मुस्लिम नाम नई पीढ़ी में विशेषकर लड़कियों में कुछ हद तक स्वीकार्य हो रहे थे। कयामत से कयामत तक की सफलता ने लव जिहाद को समाज में स्थापित करने में बड़ी भूमिका निभाई। मुस्लिम लड़के उसी फिल्मी हीरो के अंदाज में बाल रखते, कपड़े पहनते और फिर उन जगहों में प्रवेश के लिए प्रेरित हो रहे थे, जहाँ हिन्दू समाज की लड़कियाँ आती-जाती रहती या उत्सव मनाती हो। बॉलीवुड में एक और विचित्र बात उभरने लगी थी। हिन्दू अभिनेता भले ही दूसरे पायदान पर चले गए हों, लेकिन

हिन्दू लड़कियाँ विशेष कर नई-नई लड़कियों को गजब का प्रश्रय मिलने लगा था। परिणाम इस प्रकार सामने आया कि मुस्लिम हीरो, हिन्दू हिरोइन। लव-जिहाद का दौर फिल्मी दुनियाँ में जोरदार चल रहा था और उन्हीं जैसी अंदाज और अदाओं में जीने वाले युवा अर्थात् हिन्दू लड़कियों के जीवन में मुस्लिम लड़कों फिल्मी अंदाज में आकर रचने-बसने की कोशिश करने लगे। इस नए आयु वर्ग पर फिल्मों का प्रभाव पड़ा और लाखों लड़कियाँ लव जिहाद का शिकार हुई और अब भी हो रही है। एक आश्चर्यजनक बात यह हुई है कि जिस तैमूर लंग ने जिन लोगों के पूर्वजों की हत्या और बलात्कार किए, वैसे लोगों के घर में भी तैमूर को आदर्श बनाने में

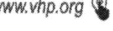

An image from the September 2020 issue of the VHP's in-house magazine.
The image of a Hindu woman transforming into a burkha-clad Muslim woman
has become a standard trope to depict 'love jihad'.

The VHP list catalogued thirty-six allegations of the concealment of religious identity by Muslim men from their Hindu partners. Let us pause for a moment to consider that number—only thirty-six cases of alleged identity deception over a nine-year period as proof of a conspiracy to alter the religious demography of a country of 1.3 billion people.

None of the thirty-six articles provided any independent proof—say, the outcome of an official investigation—to explain why a particular allegation of individual wrongdoing amounted to a larger Muslim conspiracy.

A simple Google search shows tricksters of all religious stripes exist. For instance, in February 2022, police arrested Ramesh Chandra Swain from Odisha's Kendrapara district, accused of marrying eighteen times by faking his identity.

Some of the cases of identity fraud in the VHP list did not even seem to be outright con jobs. For example, the list featured an *OpIndia* article from June 2019, in which the publication assigned, without any supporting proof, the 'love jihad' label to the case of a Muslim man who allegedly faked a Brahmin identity and married a Brahmin woman from Rajasthan. The man was arrested following a complaint by the father of the woman. An article in the *Times of India* on the same case quoted the police as saying the couple are adults, and there is little the police could do. The report cited a video released by the woman saying she was aware of her partner's religious identity and that their marriage was consensual.

OpIndia was the single largest contributor to the VHP's list, with thirty-five articles. It is a pro-Hindutva website repeatedly found carrying misinformation.

The list also relied on seven entries from the obscure website Hinduexistence.org, where the claims took an even more scurrilous turn. For instance, a Hinduexistence piece from June 2017 on the VHP list used the term 'Love Jihad plot' to describe the murder of a twenty-three-year-old Hindu woman from Chittoor, Andhra Pradesh. She was reportedly stabbed to death by her Muslim suitor when she rejected his proposal. No evidence is provided of a Muslim conspiracy other than the fantastical allegation that the murder was the result of the 'rise of testosterone...due to regular beef eating at the time of (Ramadan) fasting, creating abnormal sexual advances including sex insanity leading to rape and murder.'

The VHP list also relies on mainstream media reports—but uses some of them in a misleading way. For instance, in February 2020, *Dainik Jagran*, one of India's largest selling Hindi dailies, reported that a Hindu woman had eloped with her Muslim lover in a town in Jharkhand, and her family had labelled it a case of 'love jihad'. The headline of the report used the term 'love story'. And yet, it landed up on the VHP list.

Conclusion: The VHP list offers no evidence of a Muslim conspiracy. Instead, from the wide catchment of gender-related crimes in India, the VHP and its media allies have cherry-picked disconnected instances of accusations of violence, fraud, or misogynistic behaviour by Muslim men towards their Hindu female partners and sought to pass it off as 'love jihad'.

◆

CLAIM: 'Love jihad' is real because...Hindu women are being made to convert to Islam by their Muslim partners

The Hindu Right not only passes off individual instances of gender crimes as 'love jihad'. It also labels cases where Hindu women converted to Islam to marry Muslim partners as proof of the conspiracy.

But are they?

In 2021, we met Fiza Fatima, earlier Shalini Yadav, and

her partner Faizal in Delhi. The couple lived in Kanpur, but had fled to Delhi after finding themselves in the centre of a firestorm. They were among fourteen supposed cases of 'love jihad' investigated by the Uttar Pradesh police, all from the same neighbourhood in Kanpur.

Fiza, who was twenty-two when we met her, rubbished the suggestion that she had been hoodwinked by her partner.

'I am pursuing an MBA. I am well-educated. Do I look like someone who can be lured so easily?' she asked. 'Am I a little baby girl that I can be brainwashed?'

She said her relationship with Faizal is 'love, which they are calling "jihad"'.

The testimonies of several other Hindu women we spoke to was similar—they all said their choice of partners and the decision to convert were entirely their own. Our report went viral.

Many on social media were supportive of the couples. But we were also flooded with questions like these:

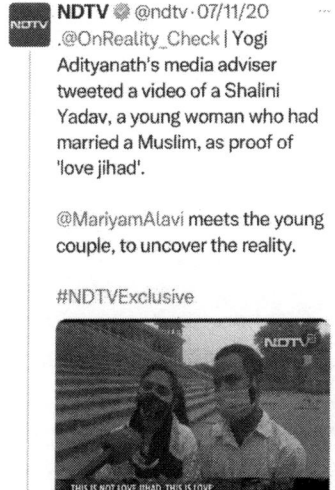

NDTV ✅ @ndtv · 07/11/20 ···
.@OnReality_Check | Yogi Adityanath's media adviser tweeted a video of a Shalini Yadav, a young woman who had married a Muslim, as proof of 'love jihad'.

@MariyamAlavi meets the young couple, to uncover the reality.

#NDTVExclusive

THIS IS NOT LOVE JIHAD, THIS IS LOVE

♡ 412   ↻ 1,930   ♡ 6,279   ﹗   ⬆

Kiran ···
@Kjeet978

If the muslim boy really loves a hindu girl, then why not marry her as a hindu only??? Why convert ???

Rani ···
@Rani64852905

The question is y the conversion for marriage ??

Lipun Kumar ···
@LipunKu30541876

Love marriage is ok but why is the conversion ? Is it necessary? And if it then converse both to another religion or dont change. I know you have every rights but these things looks odd.

Some of these Twitter posts may reflect genuine confusion, even concern over the trend of Hindu women converting to Islam. But the Hindu Right, scrambling to produce evidence for its claims of a large-scale conspiracy, projects these cases as forced conversions.

When we asked Fiza, she told us there was no pressure on her to convert. In fact, the decision on who would convert was made on the spur of the moment.

Faizal said, 'When we went to get married, they asked who is converting, I said I will.'

Fiza interrupted him then to say: 'I am converting.'

'I told her you don't know what can happen,' Faisal recalled. 'We need to get married, so I will get converted. She said no.'

Fiza continued: 'I took him to the side and said why will you convert? I want to.'

This back and forth finally culminated in Fiza converting to Islam.

But why convert at all?

Their answer: to avoid the risk of getting entangled with the provisions of the Special Marriage Act, a law inextricably linked to the 'love jihad' theory. Enacted in 1954, the law was meant to enable secular marriages, particularly of interfaith couples wanting to tie the knot without either having to convert. In contrast, to marry under religion-based personal laws, either the man or the woman would have to convert to the religion of their partner.

But the Special Marriage Act has a stipulation that couples must give a thirty-day advance notice of their marriage, to be pasted in a prominent place, say, in the offices of the registrar. The notices have become homing beacons for Hindutva groups and aggrieved families to discover and disrupt such alliances.

Entire anti-'love jihad' ecosystems have sprung up to scour notice boards in district offices for notices under the Special

Marriage Act, using the findings to harass couples.

Social media has increased the risks. It is commonplace to find marriage notices being posted online, accompanied by calls for vigilante intervention. In April 2022, a marriage notification of a Delhi-based Muslim man to a Hindu woman was posted on a Facebook page called 'Modi-Yogi Samarthako ka manch', or the platform of supporters of Prime Minister Modi and UP Chief Minister Adityanath. The post asked local Hindu groups to stop what it called 'Nikah Jihad'.

But it isn't just vigilante groups that interfaith couples must worry about. A new threat has been added to the mix.

In October 2020, speaking at a rally in Jaunpur ahead of bye-elections in the state, the chief minister of Uttar Pradesh, Yogi Adityanath, issued a dire warning against 'love jihad': 'I warn those who conceal identity and play with our sisters' respect. If you don't mend your ways, your 'Ram naam satya yatra'—funeral procession will begin.'

Less than a year later, the UP government passed the Uttar Pradesh Prohibition of Unlawful Conversion of Religion Act, placing restrictions on conversion by or for marriage.

In the next eighteen months, four other states—Gujarat, Madhya Pradesh, Haryana, and Karnataka—passed similar laws, or updated their existing anti-conversion laws. Uttarakhand and Himachal Pradesh had passed similar laws before Uttar Pradesh.

To be clear, anti-conversion laws, passed in response to (often exaggerated) anxieties over unlawful conversions, have a long history in India. We tackle the chilling effect of these laws in more detail in a subsequent chapter. To sum up, these laws frame unlawful conversions in the broadest possible terms— misrepresentation, force, inducement, allurement, deception— categories vague enough to render any change of religion illegal. Now, in the era of 'love jihad', to this long list has been added a clause making conversion by marriage or for marriage unlawful.

Arvind Singh
27 April 2022 · 🌐

🔴 निकाह जिहाद @ दिल्ली...!

दिल्ली के हिंदू संगठन कृपया ध्यान दें..!

सहयोगियों के द्वारा प्राप्त सूचना के अनुसार 49 साल का जसोला, दिल्ली निवासी प्रौढ़ लव-जिहादी ▓▓▓▓▓ ▓▓▓▓ ▓▓▓▓ 18 साल की हिंदू बच्ची के साथ निकाह करने जा रहा है।

मालूम हुआ है कि इसकी पहली बीबी भी हिंदू है। यह ट्यूशन पढ़ाकर कम उम्र की हिंदू बच्चियों को फंसाता है और फिर उनका यौन शोषण करता है।

दिल्ली के हिंदू संगठनों से आग्रह है कि वे तत्काल प्रभाव से इस इस्लामी आतंकवादी को जूतामाइसीन का हाहाकारी डोज अता करें और उसके बाद इसका डीपेस्ट तरीके से पूर्णरूपेण खतना मुक्कम्मल अता फरमाने की ज़हमत उठाएं।

शलोऊँ...!

–बाबा इज़रायली ✡

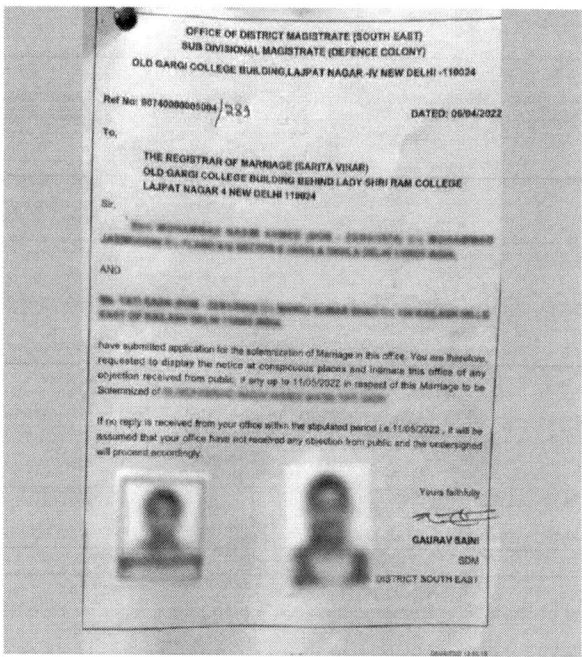

👍💬 31   5 comments   35 shares

A notice by an interfaith couple under the Special Marriage Act was publicized
on social media in order to disrupt their wedding plans. We have redacted the
personal details of the couple, out of respect for their privacy.

It is a watershed, if bizarre, moment in the journey of 'love jihad'—an unproven, divisive theory has moved from the fringe to being passed into the actual statute.

The term 'love jihad' doesn't feature anywhere in the laws. But the language of the laws closely mimics the Hindu Right's line on 'love jihad'—that Muslims are concealing their identity to dupe and convert Hindu women.

Take this excerpt from the Statements of Objects and Reasons from the anti-conversion law passed by Uttarakhand:

> We have come across incidents in which with an agenda to increase strength of their own religion by getting people from other religions converted to their own religion, people do marry girls of other religions by misrepresentation of their own religion and after getting marriage to such girls, they get them converted to their own religion.

We examined seven state laws. We found that, in effect, they criminalize conversion for marriage, reverse the burden of proof, and in some states, mandate a sixty-day notice period for those converting, widening the scope of the harassment of interfaith couples.

Some of the laws are facing judicial pushback.

In August 2021, the Gujarat High Court while hearing a petition challenging the state's anti-'love jihad' law, stayed the clause making interfaith marriages a means of forceful conversion, saying it 'interferes with the intricacies of marriage including the right to the choice of an individual, thereby infringing Article 21 of the Constitution of India.'

In November 2021, in response to a petition challenging the Uttar Pradesh law, the Allahabad High Court said that a marriage registrar cannot refuse to register marriages by citing the absence of prior approval of authorities to the conversion.

In November 2022, the Madhya Pradesh High Court in an interim order held that the sections of the anti-conversion law in the state which required prior notice to the authorities regarding conversions were unconstitutional. In response to the state's plea before the Supreme Court, the apex court said: 'All conversions cannot be said to be illegal'.

CONCLUSION: Hindu-Muslim couples are caught in a pincer. A provision in the Special Marriage Act enables vigilantism, and is forcing them to opt for religious conversion. New anti-conversion laws are criminalizing the act.

◆

CLAIM: 'Love jihad' is real because...people are getting arrested under the new laws

While the legal challenges to anti-'love jihad' laws grind on in the courts, on the ground, the consequences are already playing out. States are using the laws to crack down on interfaith couples, arresting the Muslim male partners of Hindu women. But as we found out through Right to Information requests, the police often have only a hazy idea of the 'crime' at hand.

We filed several Right to Information requests with the union Home Ministry and all seven states which had passed 'love jihad' laws, as well as states in which prominent political functionaries had made claims about 'love jihad'. Several states rejected our RTI requests outright. Others passed down our queries to the district level.

We began by asking the authorities to provide us with the legal definition of 'love jihad'. The answers from the centre and the states typically ranged from 'no information available' to 'not the competent authority to reply', and 'no legal definition' of 'love jihad'.

A response from the Superintendent of Police, Guwahati, Assam, was revelatory: it said while 'love jihad' is not defined under law, it is a 'term commonly used to describe [the] marital relationship between Muslim men and Hindu women'. In other words, in the eyes of law enforcement, the mere fact of a Muslim man being in a relationship with a Hindu woman amounts to an Islamic conspiracy.

We also asked the centre and the states to disclose how many cases of 'love jihad' had occurred in the last ten years, and whether the number was large enough to necessitate the passage of laws to combat the supposed menace. This, too, was met with a series of non-responses.

Only one district provided specific information. A police department response from Ambala, Haryana, said between 2019 and 2022, the district had seen seventeen marriages where the couples got married after one of them converted. It is unclear how this establishes a conspiracy, let alone justifies the passage of the Haryana anti-conversion law in 2022.

We also asked the states to provide information on cases filed under their anti-conversion laws.

Uttar Pradesh was the only state that put down a considerable number. It said that between November 2020 and May 2022, the state had filed 206 cases under the anti-conversion law—a staggering figure. But the state did not spell out how many of these were related to conversion for marriage. Nor did it provide any case specific information—for instance, first information report (FIR) numbers—hobbling any chances of independent inquiry.

A year later, the number of cases registered under the law had further gone up, according to a press statement released by the UP government in May 2023. It said the police had registered 427 cases and made 833 arrests under the new law between January 2021 and April 2023. We followed up by filing another RTI request with Uttar Pradesh, asking for case specific details, but received no reply.

In the absence of official information, we did the next best thing: we scoured through news coverage, looking for case details. We found reports on twenty-three cases registered under the new law, till October 2022. These included cases of conversion related to marriage, as well as conversion of a general nature. We focused on the former.

After organizing the list chronologically, we investigated the first five cases, all of which appeared to have been registered within days of the UP law coming into force.

CASE 1: JIBRAIL AND NEETU, SITAPUR DISTRICT

On 26 November 2020, Sarvesh Shukla, the father of Neetu, nineteen, filed a police complaint alleging his daughter had been kidnapped by Jibrail, twenty-four, their Muslim neighbour. The complaint made no mention of forced conversion. UP's anti-conversion law had not come into effect. It would—two days later.

Even the kidnapping charge appeared baseless. Neetu's parents, when we met them in June 2023, themselves conceded their daughter had eloped of her own volition. Their outrage came from her choice of partner. 'Jibrail is a behna, we are pandits,' Neetu's mother, Rekha Shukla, told us. Behna is the name of a Muslim community in parts of northern and western India. Pandits are Brahmins, the same caste as the Shuklas. 'It is of great shame if a girl goes with a behna,' the mother said. 'Even if she had died, it would have been okay but she could not have stayed with him.'

The father added, 'If she had eloped with a Brahmin, we ourselves would have asked her to marry him.'

But since Jibrail was Muslim, they went to the police instead.

The parents said the police were initially unhelpful and so they contacted local Hindutva groups. 'I called Uttam Singh of the Bajrang Dal,' Sarvesh Shukla recalled. 'That's when these people helped in putting pressure.'

Singh told us he was a district-level staff manager for the Dal. He boasted that the police cracked down only after his outfit intervened.

In a matter of days, the charge of forced conversion— passed into law on 28 November—was added to the FIR. 'I don't know how,' Sarvesh Shukla told us. 'I am not educated.'

The police arrested thirteen of Jibrail's relatives and Muslim neighbours. Three months later, Neetu and Jibrail handed themselves over to the police. 'Jibrail's house had been sealed. Everyone was arrested. That's why they surrendered,' Deepti Singh, a constable at the police station overseeing the case, said.

Jibrail, too, was arrested and sent to a local jail. Initially, Neetu appeared before the police and a local magistrate to say that she had willingly gone with Jibrail, a man she was in love with, and that she had chosen to change her religion to be with him. But soon after, she gave a fresh statement saying she was forcibly converted.

On paper, Neetu may have altered—or been made to alter—her position. But her emotions were unchanged. Her parents said she was frenzied at being separated from Jibrail. 'She had gone completely mad. She smashed her head on the wall of the police station,' Neetu's mother said. Neetu was eventually moved to a government-run women's home in Lucknow. According to Aarti Singh, superintendent of the home, it took months of 'counselling' to convince Neetu that a relationship with a Muslim man is a mistake. 'We scolded her, made her understand. What is so great about Jibrail? His name is also strange. Do you even know his family properly?'

Singh said. 'We told her in their community they can have multiple marriages.'

Eight months later, Neetu returned home. On the advice of the police, her parents immediately married her into a Hindu family. 'They own land. They have an income of ₹50,000–60,000 from tent-making. They don't know about what happened with Neetu,' her father said.

Jibrail and the thirteen other accused eventually got bail. According to Mohammed Akib, a neighbour and a co-accused, Jibrail now sells mangoes in Lucknow: 'He has to feed himself somehow.'

CASE 2: UVAISH AND ASHA, BAREILLY DISTRICT

On the day the anti-conversion law came into effect, Tikaram, a farmer, registered a police complaint against Uvaish Ahmed, a Muslim man from his village. He said Uvaish, twenty, and his daughter, Asha, nineteen, knew each other since school, and that Uvaish was pressuring Asha to convert and marry him. The police arrested Uvaish under a raft of charges, including for breach of peace. They also booked him under the anti-conversion law.

In court, Uvaish's lawyers argued there was no evidence against him, and that the police complaint mentioned no date of the alleged crime. Less than a month after his arrest, the court granted him bail.

In an interview, Uvaish told us that he had known Asha since school, where they had been classmates and friends. 'There was no relationship as such. But we did talk on the phone at times,' he said. He linked his arrest to an earlier episode from 2019, when Asha went missing. At the time, too, the police had arrested Uvaish based on a complaint by her family that he had kidnapped her. In a statement to the court, Asha, who eventually returned home, said she had left home of her own volition, and that Uvaish had nothing to do with it. Uvaish was released. A year later, Asha married a Hindu man.

Since the 2019 episode, Uvaish said he has had no contact with Asha. He suspected the police, aware of the earlier case, had pressured her family to book him under the new law.

A police official we contacted at the station where the complaint was registered said he did not have details of the case.

Tikaram, Asha's father, seemed unclear about his own complaint against Uvaish, first telling us he did not file it, later saying he did.

Uvaish said the state was 'putting false cases on everyone and keeping them in jail under these laws…. It's just to ruin our lives.'

CASE 3: NADEEM AND PARUL, MUZAFFARNAGAR DISTRICT

A day after the UP anti-conversion law came into force, Akshay Kumar Tyagi, a Haridwar-based contractor, filed a case in his hometown, Muzaffarnagar, against a labourer who worked for him. Tyagi alleged Nadeem, twenty-seven, had begun an illicit relationship with his wife, Parul, and was attempting to convert her. However, Parul told the police she knew Nadeem, but did not have any relationship with him. She alleged that her husband had falsely implicated Nadeem because he had supported her when she faced domestic violence and 'mental torture'.

The case unravelled swiftly.

In December 2020, three weeks after the police registered the case, the Allahabad High Court gave Nadeem protection from arrest, saying: 'There is no material before us that any force or coercive process is being adopted by the petitioner (Nadeem) to convert (Parul). Victim is admittedly an adult who understands her well being. She as well as the petitioner have a fundamental right to privacy and being grown up adults who are aware of the consequences of their alleged relationship.'

A month later, the court recorded that the state itself had dropped charges under the anti-conversion law. Nadeem is out on bail, but is being prosecuted under other sections, including criminal intimidation, breach of peace, and criminal conspiracy—for a crime that Parul, the alleged victim, says he did not commit.

CASE 4: SHABAB AND AYUSHI, MAU DISTRICT

In December 2020, Shabab Khan, thirty-eight, was arrested by the police after his former employer, Premchand Seth, accused him of kidnapping and attempting to convert his daughter, Ayushi, thirty, on the eve of her marriage. Shabab used to work in Seth's house as a driver.

According to Seth's complaint, Shabab and his family were part of an 'active gang' involved in 'love jihad'. Shabab and thirteen of his relatives and friends, including his wife, were slapped with multiple charges, including under the anti-conversion law.

But Shabab and his family tell a very different story. His sister, Fatima, said Shabab was in a long-running affair with Ayushi, something he concealed from his family. When Ayushi's family pressured her into marrying a Hindu man, the two decided to elope. Shabab told us he and Ayushi fled to Kolkata, where they got married at a Kali temple according to Hindu rituals.

Far from the marriage being a case of so-called 'love jihad'—a Muslim man forcing a Hindu woman to convert to Islam—Shabab said he converted to Hinduism, renaming himself Rahul Khan. 'Till date I continue to follow Hindu rituals. I keep a fast on Tuesday for Bajrangbali,' he said. Even the police complaint by Ayushi's father and court documents refer to him as 'Shabab Khan aka Rahul Khan'.

Shabab showed us a photo of the two of them soon after they got married, but asked us not to publish it. In the image, the couple can be seen seated in the back of a car, smiling into the camera. Ayushi has sindoor in the parting of her hair, and is wearing a mangalsutra—the adornments of a Hindu bride.

Back in the custody of her family after a team from UP police brought the couple back from Kolkata, Ayushi told a judge that she had been 'enticed away' by Shabab. She said at his request, she had given him ₹3.3 lakhs in cash and 250-300 grams of gold jewellery. Shabab denied this, claiming Ayushi's well-connected and wealthy family had used their clout to falsely implicate him. 'You can do a lot of things with money,' he said.

Today, all the accused, including Shabab, are out on bail. In the bail order, the judge noted 'the modesty of the victim has not been outraged, her religion has not been changed (and) the applicant does not possess any criminal history'.

Ayushi and her family were not available for comment.

Umesh Yadav, the investigating officer of the case, insisted Shabab had duped Ayushi. When we asked how, he said: 'The two of them used to speak. Wohi toh behlana fuslana hua. That is what manipulation is.'

CASE 5: AZAD AND UNNAMED WOMAN, HARDOI DISTRICT

The charges against Mohammed Azad, a resident of Hardoi, were serious—under the pretext of marriage, he had not just attempted to forcibly convert a Hindu woman, but had also raped her.

But court documents underscore the holes in the police case.

In a statement to the magistrate, recorded in a trial court order, the woman made no mention of rape, nor of forced conversion. She said she had known Azad for several years, and was in a relationship with him, against her parents' wishes. They were planning to get married in a court in Shahabad, a nearby town, when Azad asked her to convert to Islam. When she refused, Azad dropped her back to Hardoi.

A slightly different version of these events was reported at the time the case had first surfaced: Azad and the young woman had gone to the court to get married under the Special Marriage Act, but her father had appeared at the last moment, and the plan had failed. From a groom-to-be, Azad found himself in jail, facing rape charges. A police officer told a reporter: 'It is a fact that the two were in love. She knew that he was a Muslim and went to the court to marry him. Now that we received a complaint of forceful conversion, we registered the case and made the arrest.'

During Azad's bail proceedings, the prosecution did not press the charge of rape, a point highlighted by Azad's lawyer and summarized by the judge: 'It is not the prosecution case that forcibly physical relationship has been made... It is next contended that it is a consensual relationship between two persons. No case for rape is made out. The medical report does not corroborate the prosecution story.'

Granting Azad bail, the judge noted that the government

lawyer opposed the bail plea but could not 'dispute the aforesaid facts' argued by Azad's counsel.

So how did a Muslim man in a consensual relationship with a Hindu woman end up as an accused?

A likely answer: Hindutva groups.

Pawan Rastogi, the district coordinator of the Hardoi unit of the Bajrang Dal, told us he had been in touch with the young woman's family. 'I went with her parents to get the girl back,' he said. Rastogi claimed he had helped the woman's family file the police complaint, implicating Azad.

In December 2020, while speaking with a reporter, Rastogi had been even more boastful. 'Hum inko jihad failane nahi denge—We will not let Muslims spread jihad,' he had said. His confidence stemmed from the newly-passed anti-conversion law. 'Thanks to the law, we can operate freely.'

CONCLUSION: Scores of arrests are happening under the new 'love jihad' laws. But a close examination of cases filed in Uttar Pradesh showed no evidence of conspiracy. The latest threat to interfaith couples is not from vigilante groups or aggrieved families, but from the all-powerful Indian state.

Postscript: In response to our RTIs looking for evidence of forced conversions, we came across a case from Jharkhand, involving allegations of a Muslim woman being forced to convert to Hinduism. According to the police FIR from Gumla, dated November 2020, a Muslim woman from Assam, Abida Begum, alleged that a Hindu man named Buddhdev Thakur married her by pretending to be a Muslim. Four years later, she discovered he was Hindu, and was already married. She said he forced her to convert to Hinduism, and attempted to kill her when she refused. Reverse 'love jihad', anyone?

Chapter 2

'POPULATION JIHAD'

Of all the theories we tackle in the book, this is perhaps the oldest—a Muslim conspiracy to reduce India's Hindus to a minority through a population explosion.

The argument goes back more than 100 years. It was the subject of a book published in 1909 called *A Dying Race* by Lieutenant Colonel Upendro Nath Mukerji, an Indian Medical Service officer who went on to become an influential figure in the nascent Hindu Right movement. Mukerji compared the disappearance of indigenous populations under colonial rule in countries like New Zealand to the situation of Hindus in Bengal. 'We are also a decaying race,' he wrote. 'Every census reveals the same fact. We are getting proportionately fewer and fewer. There is no actual decrease; but the rate of increase compared with that of the Mahomedans is extremely small'.

After ninety-seven pages of analysis, he concluded: 'The Mohamedans have a future and they believe in it. We Hindus have no conception of it... They are growing in number, growing in strength, growing in wealth, growing in solidarity, we are crumbling to pieces. They look forward to a united Mohamedan world—we are waiting for our extinction.'

Over a century later, Hindus are far from extinct. India alone has nearly a billion of them.

Hindus make up 79.80 per cent of the country's population, with 966 million people, according to the last Census. Muslims account for 14.23 per cent, with 172 million people.

And yet, the threat posed by supposed Muslim overbreeding continues to loom large in the Hindutva universe, frequently raised by top political leaders.

For instance, in 2002, Narendra Modi, then chief minister of Gujarat, had called relief camps housing Muslim families fleeing religious violence 'child producing centres'. Two decades later, Uttar Pradesh chief minister Yogi Adityanath, without naming any community, said: 'It should not be the case that the population growth rate and share of a particular group should continue to increase, while the population of mool nivasi (original inhabitants) is stabilised through awareness and enforcement programmes.' Such population stabilization is 'a matter of worry for any country', he argued, since it 'has a negative impact on religious demography and after a while chaos and anarchy is created'.

Other wings of the Hindutva ecosystem have been more explicit—the RSS-affiliated publication, *Organiser*, in a 2021 piece accused Muslims of carrying out 'population jihad':

> The doctrine of Islam is based upon the total Islamisation of the world; there should not be a single non–Muslim left over before the Jihad ends. With such a philosophy in mind, increasing population is one of the forms of Jihad. Whereas the entire world is limiting the family size, only Muslims are growing at an alarming pace. So, the Population Jihad is real and ticking...

And, of course, social media is where 'population jihad' is repurposed for the WhatsApp forward era. Online posts about an uncontrolled rise in Muslim population are often accompanied by pictures of large Muslim families—pictures that sometimes aren't even from India. For instance, an image of a Muslim man riding a scooter with six family members circulated widely before fact checkers traced its origin to Bangladesh.

A. Soni
@ashutoshsoni888   ...

Kagaz nhi dikhayege |
Par population badayge |
Subsidy hum khayege |
Our last m Hum Dhekenge |

9:14 AM · Jan 18, 2020

4 Retweets **1** Quote **36** Likes

A social media post highlighting Muslim population increase
in India, by a user who identifies as a BJP member.
Fact checkers traced this image to Bangladesh.

Not that such debunking makes a difference to the proponents
of the Muslim takeover theory. For them, even large Muslim
families in Bangladesh pose a danger to India. This is because
the thesis of Hindu supremacists doesn't just rest on the claim
of a planned population explosion by Indian Muslims, but on
the related assertion that Muslims from India's neighbouring

countries are crossing borders illegally. Together, they argue, this will soon lead to Hindus getting outnumbered by Muslims.

Does either claim measure up?

◆

CLAIM: 'Population jihad' is real...because Muslim growth rate is off the charts

If we go purely by census numbers, the idea that 172 million Muslims can overwhelm close to a billion Hindus in the not too distant future may seem fantastical.

The Hindu Right has a response to this—which also relies on the Census and other government data.

Their argument goes something like this: yes, Hindus today are about 79.80 per cent of the population. But historical census data shows a higher Hindu figure dropping over the years even as Muslim numbers increased. The reason—Muslims have a higher fertility rate compared to Hindus.

The bare facts of the argument are undeniable. The census of 1951, the first such exercise after India gained independence, recorded India's Hindu population share at 84.98 per cent, and Muslims' share at 9.91 per cent.

Sixty years later, the 2011 census showed India's Hindu population share had slipped below 80 per cent for the first time, while the share of Muslim population had risen to 14.23 per cent in the same period.

Figure 2.1

The share of Hindus in India's population slipped below 80% in 2011

Hindu population, in percentage

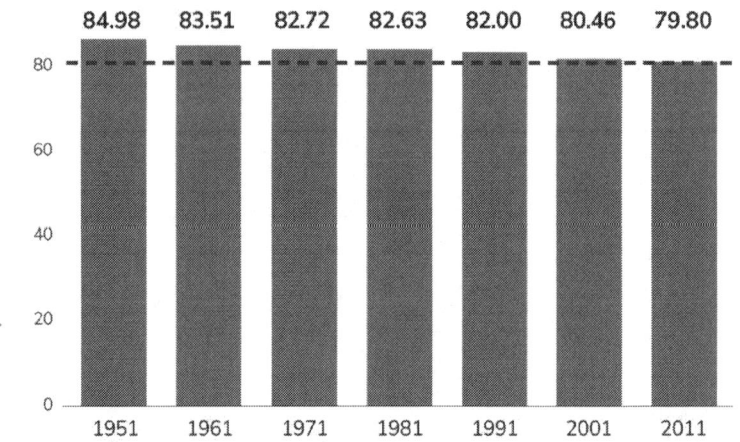

Source: Census of India

Between 1951 and 2011, the Muslim population did grow faster than Hindus. Muslims grew by 386.37 per cent, while Hindus grew by 218.29 per cent.

The claim of a higher Muslim fertility rate is also true. Fertility rate measures the average number of children born to women through their reproductive years. The last round of the National Family and Health Survey conducted in 2019-20 found the Muslim fertility rate (2.36) was 42 decimal points higher than the Hindu rate (1.94). Simply put, this means Muslim women are having more children than Hindu women.

Armed with these numbers, Hindutvavadis claim Muslims will overrun Hindus in the near future—the successful culmination of 'population jihad'.

Go back a few decades, and this argument falls apart.

A mass of data tells us the growth rates of all communities are falling, including that of Muslims. Between the last two census rounds, the Hindu population growth rate came down from 20.35 per cent to 16.76 per cent, while that of Muslims fell more sharply from 36.02 per cent to 24.65 per cent. Even when it comes to fertility rates, the gap between Hindus and Muslims has been steadily narrowing, a trend visible ever since data from large surveys became available in the early 1990s. In fact, the Muslim fertility rate is coming down faster than the Hindu fertility rate, as Figure 2.2 shows.

In demographic circles, this has led to the general consensus that the growth rates of both communities will eventually converge, with their respective populations stabilizing not too far from existing levels.

A widely cited forecast was made by P. N. Mari Bhat, one of India's most distinguished demographers and the former director of the International Institute of Population Sciences. In 2005, Professor Bhat, along with A. J. Francis Zavier, projected that Hindus will reach a stable population by 2061, while Muslims will take another forty years, their numbers stabilizing by 2101. The Muslim share in India's population, according to him, will settle at 18.8 per cent, while the Hindu share will be about 74.7 per cent.

The Bhat-Zavier projection was seen as a counter to another one that had set off a debate in media and academic circles. It claimed that in just six decades, by 2061, Muslims and Christians would outnumber 'Indian Religionists'—a term that included not just followers of religions that originated in India, but even Parsis and Jews. So, anyone but Muslims and Christians.

Figure 2.2

The growth rate of India's Muslim population has fallen sharply in recent years...

Decadal population growth rate, in percentage

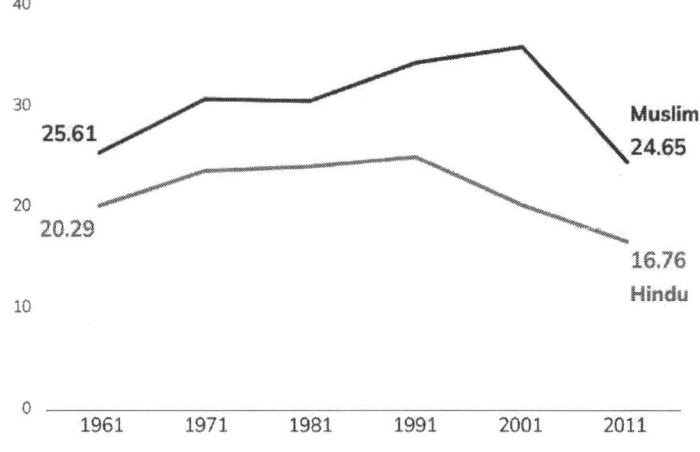

Source: Census of India

...and so has the Muslim fertility rate. The gap is closing between Hindus and Muslims

Fertility rate

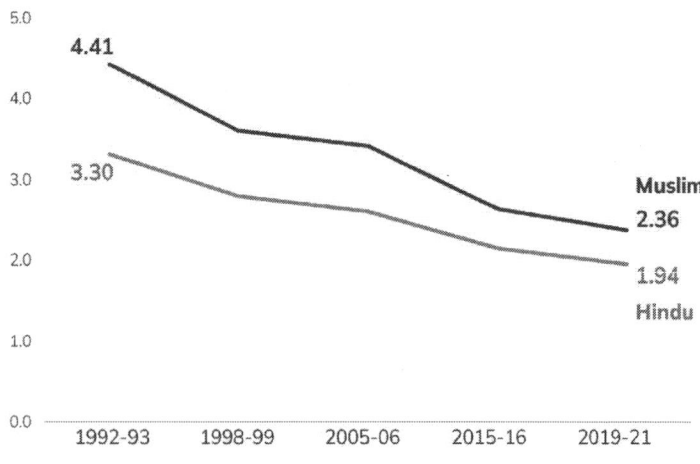

Source: National Family Health Surveys

The projection caused a stir because it was published in 2003
as part of a book that had been endorsed by then deputy
prime minister, BJP leader L. K. Advani. The Indian Council of
Social Science Research had funded the book, even though its
authors were far removed from the world of social science—
two were physicists and one was a metallurgist.

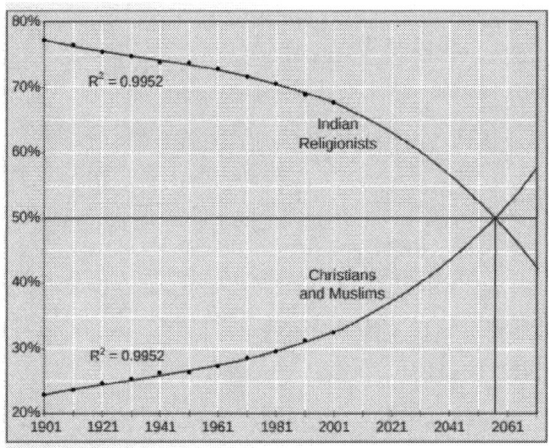

Projection by Centre for Policy Studies

Clues for why the work had attracted government support
were not hard to find: the authors were part of a Chennai-
based think tank, the Centre for Policy Studies, that counted
among its trustees key ideologues of the BJP-RSS, Balbir Punj
and S. Gurumurthy.

The starting point of the projection was itself questionable:
the definition of India included Pakistan and Bangladesh. Why
would a book published five decades after Partition make
projections pertaining to India's demographic future by clubbing
it with its former territories?

But even taking pre-Partition India as a unit—Akhand

Bharat as the Hindu Right calls it—the projection was wildly off the mark, several reviewers pointed out. Two economics professors at the Madras Institute for Development Studies applied the statistical equation used by the authors to other contexts to show it yielded ludicrous predictions—for instance, the population share of Asians in the United States, then 7 per cent, would shoot up to 50 per cent by 2140. Closer home, the share of Hindus in the population of 'India' would drop to 50.2 per cent by 2021, and by 2063, zero.

'Hindus reduced to a minority in Akhand Bharat in less than twenty years from now?!' the reviewers wrote, mockingly. 'Even staunchly paranoid patriots must be expected to blink at this prediction.'

The authors dismissed the criticism and said they stood by their projection. But two decades later, there isn't a shade of doubt that they were spectacularly wrong: Hindus are far from becoming a minority.

CONCLUSION: Muslim growth rate is higher than that of Hindus. But it is steadily coming down, because the Muslim fertility rate is dropping. These trends are available in the public domain and widely reported—except in circles that push propaganda about a 'population jihad'.

◆

CLAIM: 'Population jihad' is real...because Islam is against birth control

Muslim fertility may be decreasing, raising serious questions over the hypothesis of an Islamic mission to overtake Hindus. But Muslims still lag behind other religious groups on most family planning parameters. What could explain this?

The VHP's Alok Kumar told us it is because Muslims

'believe in procreating more children as a religious duty...in their rejection (of) population control methods'.

Asked for proof, Kumar cited Maulana Badruddin Ajmal, a Member of Parliament from Assam, as saying: 'It is the God's duty to produce children. Give us employment or not, whatever. But we will not obstruct the force of nature.'

In 2019, soon after the Assam government had proposed linking government jobs to family planning measures, Ajmal had told reporters: 'Government will not give us [Muslims] jobs anyway. I would say to our people to give birth to as many children as possible and educate them.' There was no reference to God's duty.

Ajmal is a politician with a reputation as a motormouth—not the best representative of the views of Indian Muslims on family planning.

We contacted Mohammad Salim Engineer, the vice president of Jamaat-e-Islami Hind, one of the largest Muslim organizations in India. He cited a verse from the Quran: 'Do not kill your children for fear of poverty. We provide for you and for them.'

He argued that 'not allowing children to take birth is also similar to killing them'. But he qualified that by saying: 'There's no clear ban [on contraception]. It depends on the situation and conditions.'

According to some Muslim commentators, the Quranic verse cited by Engineer has been wrongly interpreted as anti-family planning. It is actually a condemnation of infanticide.

In his book on Muslims and the population question, S. Y. Quraishi, the former chief election commissioner, said, 'Nowhere has the Quran prohibited family planning. There are only interpretations, for and against it.' Quraishi's book goes on to list examples from the ijma, or consensus of Islamic jurists, in support of family planning. 'Imam Shafei, the first contributor to the principles of Islamic jurisprudence, said that more children should not be produced if they cannot be properly supported,' Quraishi wrote.

There are divergent views among Indian Muslims on contraception, but there seems to be a greater consensus against permanent methods like sterilization.

The data bears this out.

Muslims are showing improvement in contraception usage in the last two decades, closing the gap with Hindus. Let's first look at data for married women who, according to experts, bear the main burden of contraception usage.

Contraception use among Muslim women was at 37 per cent in 1998–99. By 2019–21, it had increased to 60.20 per cent, a gain of 23.2 percentage points. The gap with Hindu women narrowed from 12.2 percentage points to 7.7 percentage points in the same period.

Strikingly, when it comes to men, contrary to perception, more Muslim men (34.10 per cent) use contraception than Hindu men (32.70 per cent).

On more permanent methods of family planning, such as female sterilization, though, Muslims continue to lag behind. In 1998–99, only 19.60 per cent of Muslim married women had undergone female sterilization as compared to 36.20 per cent of Hindu married women. Two decades later, while the rate of female sterilization among Muslims has improved to 21.80 per cent, it is still nearly half the rate of married Hindu women.

Figure 2.3

Muslim women are now using contraception nearly as much as Hindu women...

Contraception use, in percentage

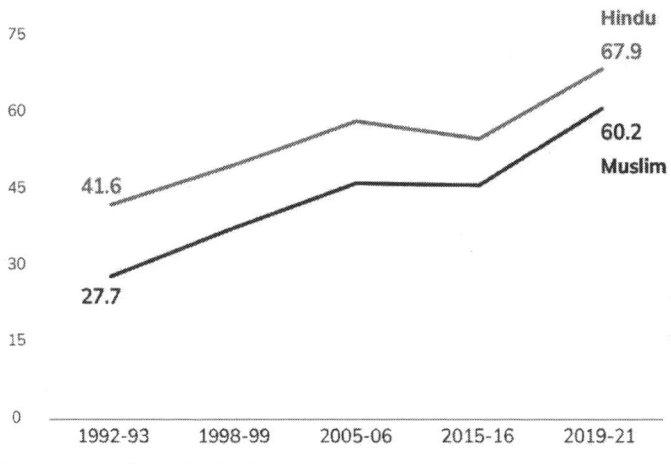

Source: National Family Health Surveys

...but on sterilization, Muslims still lag behind

sterilization, in percentage

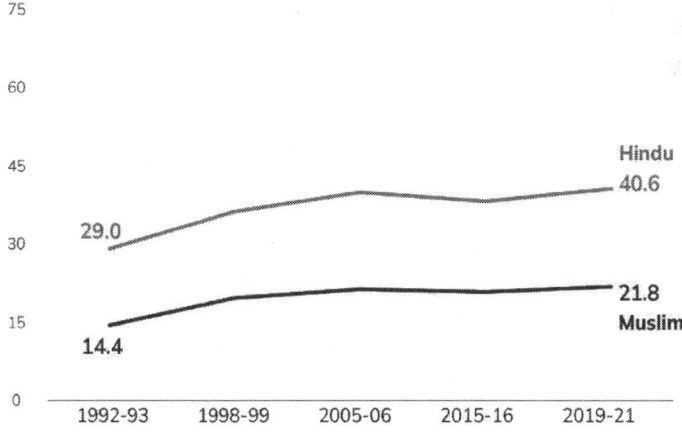

Source: National Family Health Surveys

What this suggests is that religious beliefs may have some impact on people's contraceptive choices, but not to the extent that the Hindu Right proclaims. In fact, Jammu and Kashmir and Lakshadweep, two Muslim-majority regions, have some of the lowest fertility rates in the country, significantly lower than the national average.

If not religion alone, then what? The possible answer: economics.

Bihar, one of the poorest states in India, has the highest fertility rate in the country. The average woman in Bihar is having more children than the average Muslim woman in India. So are women who have never been to school, or women who belong to the poorest 20 per cent of Indian families.

Figure 2.4

When it comes to fertility, economics matters

Fertility rate

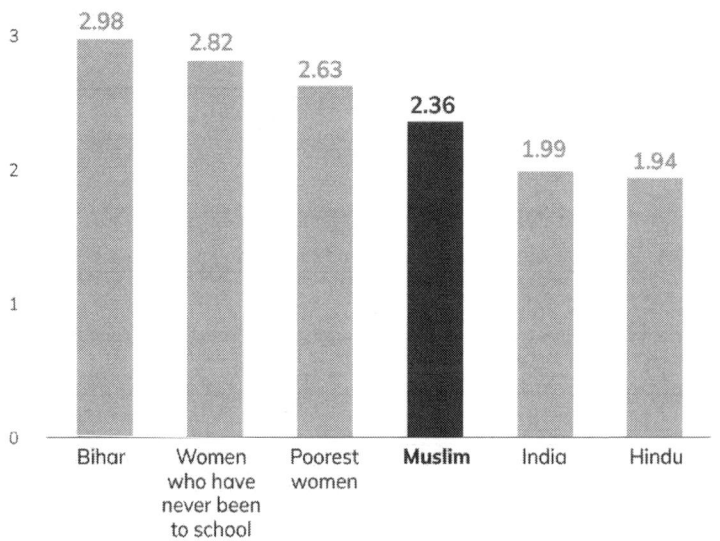

Source: National Family Health Survey 5, 2019-21

Muslims in relatively better off states of South India tend to have fertility rates lower than or comparable to the national fertility rate. In fact, Muslims in Tamil Nadu, Andhra Pradesh, and Telangana have a lower fertility rate than even Hindus in Bihar, Uttar Pradesh, and Jharkhand.

Figure 2.5

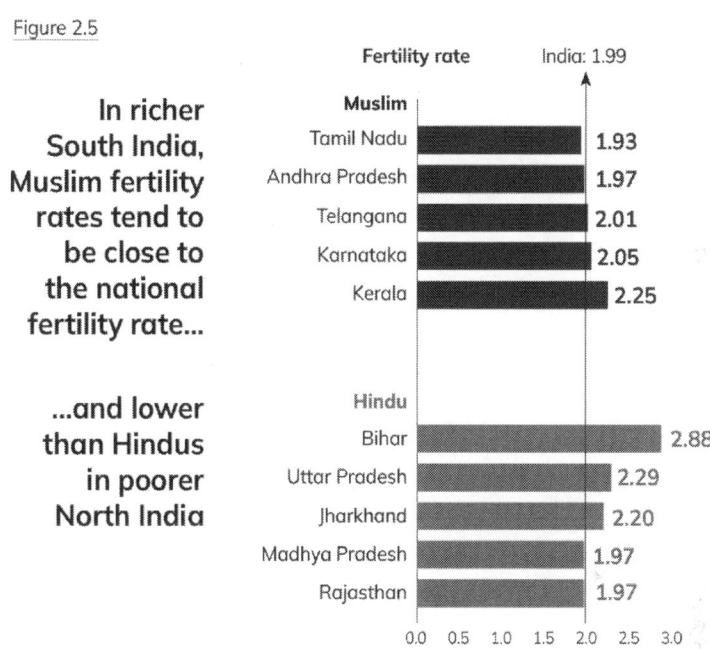

In richer South India, Muslim fertility rates tend to be close to the national fertility rate...

...and lower than Hindus in poorer North India

Fertility rate	India: 1.99
Muslim	
Tamil Nadu	1.93
Andhra Pradesh	1.97
Telangana	2.01
Karnataka	2.05
Kerala	2.25
Hindu	
Bihar	2.88
Uttar Pradesh	2.29
Jharkhand	2.20
Madhya Pradesh	1.97
Rajasthan	1.97

Source: National Family Health Survey 5, 2019-21

CONCLUSION: There is no evidence of a monolithic Islamic sanction on contraception. Income and education levels, not religious beliefs determine fertility rates. Muslims are likely to have more children because they are, on average, poorer and less educated than Hindus.

CLAIM: 'Population jihad' is real...because Muslims from neighbouring countries are infiltrating India

Muslim fertility is declining. Contraception use is up. When confronted with this data, Hindu supremacists shift goalposts. They begin to talk about the 'influx' of 'illegal migrants'.

In 2021, Pragya Thakur, a member of Parliament from the BJP, who is under trial for instigating a bombing that killed six people and injured 100 in a Muslim-majority town in Maharashtra, claimed that India was being overrun by 'Bangladeshis and Rohingyas'. The Rohingya are a Muslim minority group that fled horrific violence in Myanmar, while Bangladeshis is commonly used as a term solely for Bangladeshi Muslims. According to Thakur, they were arriving in India in hordes and 'are a burden on the country's limited resources and also aggravate the security challenges posed to the country'.

Her party president, Amit Shah, was even more vitriolic. During the 2019 election, he compared illegal immigrants to 'termites'. Months later, as India's home minister, he told Parliament that the government would prepare a National Register of Citizens to weed them out.

But when asked for data, the Home Ministry, which Shah currently heads, has been consistently evasive. Between 2014, when the Modi government first came to power and April 2023, its responses to parliamentary questions about illegal immigrants have largely stuck to the same line: we don't know.

How the Ministry of Home Affairs responded in Parliament to questions on data on illegal immigrants in India

15 July 2014
Since entry of such Bangladeshi nationals into the country (without valid travel documents) is clandestine and surreptitious, it is not possible to have accurate data of such Bangladeshi Nationals living in various parts of the country.

25 November 2014
Since entry of such Bangladeshi nationals (without valid travel documents) into the country is clandestine and surreptitious, it is not possible to have accurate data of such Bangladeshi Nationals living in various parts of the country.

22 December 2015
No correct estimate of the total number of... illegal immigrants staying in the country

6 December 2016
No confirmed data... of Bangladeshi citizens illegally residing in the country

21 March 2017
Since entry of Bangladeshi nationals into the country (without valid travel documents) is clandestine and surreptitious, accurate data of such cases is not available

11 April 2017
Since illegal immigrants enter into the country without valid travel documents in clandestine and surreptitious manner, there is no accurate data with regard to the number of Bangladeshi nationals illegally residing in the country.

1 August 2017
No accurate data with regard to their (illegal immigrants) number in the country

20 March 2018
Statistical data regarding illegal immigrants not centrally maintained.

2 July 2019
There is no accurate central data regarding exact number of such illegal immigrants.

3 March 2020
Accurate data regarding number of such (illegal) migrants living in the country, including Delhi, is not centrally maintained.

Source: Lok Sabha answers

However, in at least one response, the ministry gave a number. On 16 November 2016, the minister of state for Home, Kiren Rijiju, in reply to a question in the Rajya Sabha, reiterated the standard line—'not possible to have accurate data of such Bangladeshi nationals living in various parts of the country'. Yet, in the very next line, bewilderingly, the minister said: 'As per available inputs, there are around 20 million illegal Bangladeshi migrants staying in India.'

The contradiction undermines the credibility of the number. Besides, the minister did not specify the religion of the migrants. There is no reason to believe that migration from Bangladesh, to whatever extent it is taking place, is that of Muslims alone. In fact, there are more compelling reasons for Hindus facing religious persecution in Bangladesh to come to India.

When it comes to Rohingyas, in 2017, Rijiju said their population in India was 40,000—hardly a number that supports the claim of a Muslim invasion. Moreover, he did not specify their legal status, a curious omission given that the allegation of illegality is central to the thesis of a Muslim conspiracy.

There may be a reason for the evasiveness: while demonizing the Rohingya from the political stage, the same government appears to have quietly granted some of them quasi-legal status. In 2017, the *Indian Express* reported that 500 Rohingyas have been given long term visas by the Home Ministry, allowing them to apply for jobs, open bank accounts and seek school admission.

Lawyers working on the issue are not surprised by these double standards. In technical terms, Rohingyas in India cannot be labelled as outright illegal entrants.

To briefly explain, India has historically chosen to not be a signatory to United Nations refugee conventions which allow refugees to seek asylum in the country. Instead, refugee applications are considered under a set of guidelines issued by the central government in 2011. Under these, requests for refugee status that are 'justified on grounds of well-founded fear of persecution on account of race, religion, sex, nationality, ethnic identity' can be recommended for a Long Term Visa. This may explain why the government granted 500 such visas to Rohingyas, even as BJP leaders drummed up fears of a Rohingya 'invasion' in election campaigns.

In 2022, these double standards landed the government in a controversy. In August that year, the Minister for Housing and Urban Affairs tweeted the government's plan to provide housing and security to a group of Rohingyas in Delhi. 'India respects and follows UN Refugee Convention 1951 and provides refuge to all, regardless of their race, religion or creed,' the minister tweeted. The tweet was deleted after a political backlash, with the government clarifying that the Rohingyas in question would be held in detention centres till they are deported.

CONCLUSION: The government has provided no clear evidence to back the claims of a massive influx of illegal Muslim migrants from India's neighbouring countries.

◆

CLAIM: 'Population jihad' is real...because look at Assam

Nowhere are the anxieties of 'population jihad' more acute than in Assam, the eastern state where fears of large-scale illegal immigration and uncontrolled Muslim fertility have intersected to produce the most dire warnings of an Islamic takeover.

A commonly held belief is that Assam, which shares a long border with Bangladesh, has been swamped by Bangladeshi Muslims. An assortment of Hindutva groups and Assamese nationalists—the lines between them are increasingly getting blurred—argue that the state has an abnormal population growth rate, particularly among Muslims. Besides, they point out that Assam has the largest Muslim population share after Jammu and Kashmir and Lakshadweep. They say this couldn't have happened without immigration from Bangladesh. Ergo, 'population jihad' from across the border.

While these arguments appear to have some persuasive power, on close examination, do they hold?

Let's unpack them one by one.

DOES ASSAM HAVE AN 'ABNORMAL' POPULATION GROWTH RATE?

The answer is no, if you take a look at data from the last census.

Between 2001 and 2011, Assam's population grew by 17.07 per cent, marginally lower than India's growth rate of 17.7 per cent.

Go back forty years—the state's population growth rate has been lower than or comparable to that of India.

So where does the concern over 'abnormal' growth come from?

Go back further in time. Between 1901 and 1971, Assam's population grew at a faster pace than India's. A population surge did take place but that was 100 years ago.

Figure 2.6

For the past 50 years, Assam has been growing at a slower rate than India...

Decadal population growth rate, in percentage

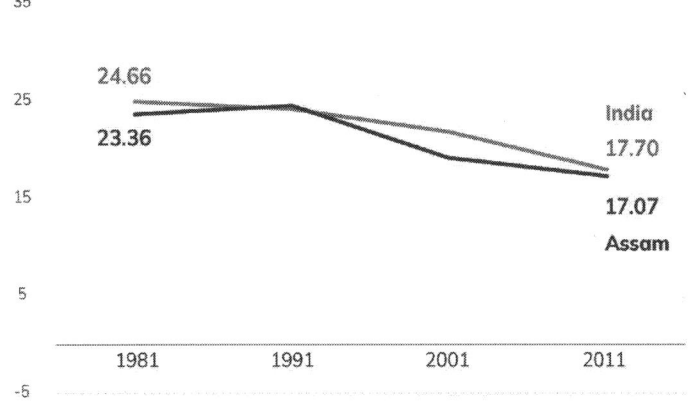

Source: Census of India

...reversing a trend that began in the colonial era

Decadal population growth rate, in percentage

Source: Census of India

What led to the surge at the turn of the century? Migration, according to Census reports.

One of the largest contingents of the migrants pouring into Assam were Muslim peasants from the district of Mymensingh in present-day Bangladesh.

By 1931, they had arrived in large enough numbers for the Census Superintendent of Assam, C. S. Mullan, to note:

> Where there is a wasteland thither flock the Mymensinghias. In fact the way in which they have seized upon the vacant areas in the Assam Valley seems almost uncanny. Without fuss, without tumult. Without undue trouble to the district revenue staff, a population which must amount to over half a million has transplanted itself from Bengal to Assam Valley during the last twenty-five years.

Is this 'population jihad' from across the border? Not quite.

Mymensingh was part of undivided Bengal—Bangladesh had not been created then. Besides, much of this migration was the outcome of colonial policies, not an Islamic conspiracy. The British encouraged farmers from undivided Bengal to move to Assam to cultivate jute in the floodplains of the Brahmaputra. They also brought Adivasis from Bihar, or present-day Jharkhand, to work in Assam's tea gardens. The mixed composition of the migrants is captured in the 1931 Census, which recorded that of the 13 lakh migrants who had entered Assam in the previous decade, 41 per cent came from Bengal, 36 per cent from Bihar and Orissa.

Although the British had themselves encouraged this migration, their officials struck a note of alarm. In 1931, Census Commissioner J. H. Hutton made an ominous observation that is cited till this date:

Prolific breeders and industrious cultivators but unruly and uncomfortable neighbours, these immigrants threaten to swamp entirely the indigenous inhabitants and in the course of two or three decades to change the whole nature, language and religion of the Brahmaputra valley.

Except, Hutton's prediction didn't quite materialize. The gap between the population growth rates of Assam and India narrowed down over the next two decades till World War II and the Partition of the country sparked another wave of migration into the state. This round of migration was harder to map.

Census reports captured the arrival of Bengali Hindus, who were fleeing Partition violence, after the Muslim majority parts of Bengal (then known as East Bengal) became part of Pakistan (known as East Pakistan). But the census superintendents noted that it was impossible to gauge the extent of the immigration since many people—in particular, Muslims—were no longer disclosing their place of birth honestly.

This could have to do with the fact that a special law, the Immigrants (Expulsion from Assam) Act, had been passed in 1950. It treated Hindu migrants from East Pakistan as 'refugees', while seeking to expel Muslim migrants as 'illegal aliens'—a policy that many criticized as unfair since Muslims, too, were caught in the throes of Partition violence.

In 1962, an even more stringent measure was introduced—the Prevention of Infiltration into India of Pakistani Nationals, (PIP) project. The government itself acknowledges that 1.78 lakh people 'were either deported or had voluntarily left' Assam between 1961–66. Their religious identity is not known. But there is wide agreement among scholars that those expelled in the 1960s were Muslim. They cite two reasons. One, as noted before, Hindu migrants had legal protection as refugees. Two, between 1961–71, the Muslim population growth rate in Assam dropped below the Hindu rate.

Figure 2.7

In Assam, the Muslim population has grown more rapidly than Hindus...

Compound annual growth rate, in percentage

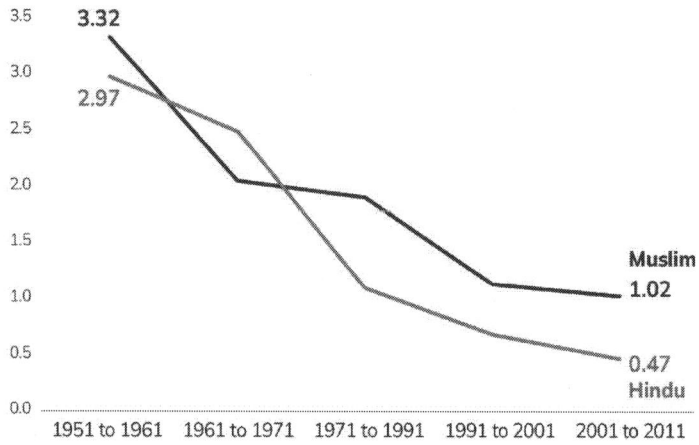

Source: Census of India

...but its Muslim growth rate isn't much different from India's

Compound annual growth rate, in percentage

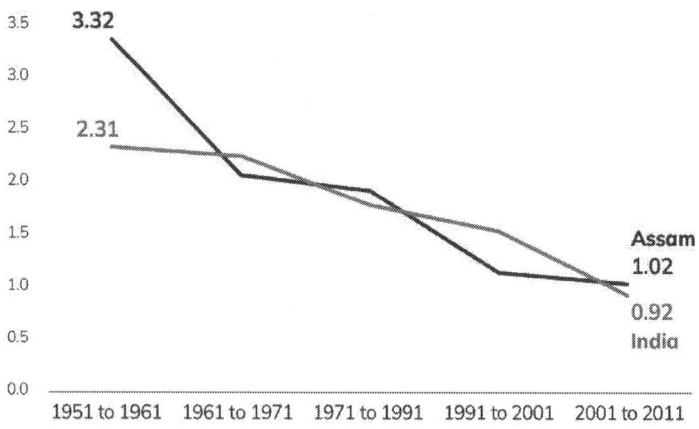

Note: Census data was not collected for Assam in 1981.
Source: Census of India

In the decades since 1971, the Muslim population growth rate in Assam has been higher than the Hindu growth rate. In Hindutva circles, this is often cited as proof of a Muslim influx from Bangladesh. But this is a weak argument: across all Indian states, Muslim growth rates tend to be higher than Hindu growth rates, an outcome of higher fertility among Muslims.

The real question is: how does Assam's Muslim growth rate compare to the rest of India?

DOES ASSAM HAVE AN 'ABNORMAL' MUSLIM GROWTH RATE?

At the start of the twentieth century, Assam's Muslim population grew at a rate higher than India's—a fact attributable to the migration of Bengali Muslim farmers into Assam.

But post-independence, the gap between the Muslim population growth rates of India and Assam has narrowed. In fact, during the 1991–2001 decade, Assam's Muslim population growth rate even slipped below India's.

Further proof that Assam's Muslim population growth rate isn't exceptional can be found in a book titled *Infiltration: Genesis of the Assam Movement* written by Abdul Mannan, a professor at Gauhati University.

Mannan compared the population growth of Muslims in Assam during 1971–1991 with Muslims in other states. The results were astonishing: several states had a higher Muslim population growth than Assam.

We did the same exercise for 2001–11. The results were similar: ten states and three union territories saw a higher growth rate of Muslims than Assam.

Figure 2.8

Assam's Muslim population growth rate is lower than that of several states

Compound annual growth rate, in percentage

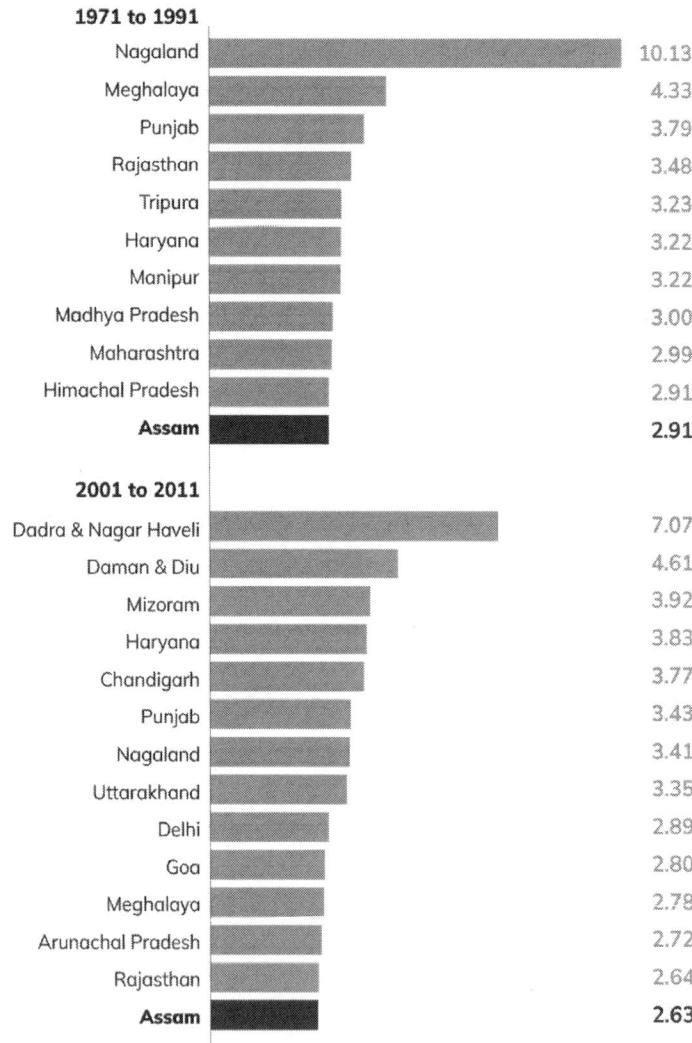

1971 to 1991

Nagaland	10.13
Meghalaya	4.33
Punjab	3.79
Rajasthan	3.48
Tripura	3.23
Haryana	3.22
Manipur	3.22
Madhya Pradesh	3.00
Maharashtra	2.99
Himachal Pradesh	2.91
Assam	**2.91**

2001 to 2011

Dadra & Nagar Haveli	7.07
Daman & Diu	4.61
Mizoram	3.92
Haryana	3.83
Chandigarh	3.77
Punjab	3.43
Nagaland	3.41
Uttarakhand	3.35
Delhi	2.89
Goa	2.80
Meghalaya	2.78
Arunachal Pradesh	2.72
Rajasthan	2.64
Assam	**2.63**

Note: Census data was not collected for Assam in 1981.

Source: Infiltration: Genesis of the Assam Movement, by Abdul Mannan (1971 to 1991); Census of India (2001 to 2011)

Where does this leave the infiltration claim?

With statewide data not supporting its argument, the Hindu Right zooms into Assam's border districts, which it claims have exceptionally high population growth rates, courtesy illegal Muslim migration.

This is also not quite true. The districts reporting higher Muslim population growth rates aren't located anywhere near the Bangladesh border.

If not immigration, what explains Assam's growing Muslim population?

A more plausible answer: fertility rates. Like in other states, Muslims in Assam have a higher fertility rate than Hindus. However, since they make up a third of Assam's population—a larger population share compared to other states—the higher fertility translates into a bigger jump in numbers.

As we explained earlier, fertility is influenced by social and economic development. The surest way to bring down Muslim fertility rates is by helping the community advance. But, tragically, Assam's Muslims continue to be demonized, particularly the descendants of migrants from pre-Partition Bengal. Even though their ancestors moved to Assam more than a century ago, they are still viewed with suspicion and routinely hauled up before foreigner tribunals that have been set up by the state to scrutinize and weed out undocumented migrants.

So strong are the fears of outsiders swamping Assam that the state recently conducted a massive exercise to sift between citizens and illegal immigrants. It asked 32.9 million of its residents to furnish proof that they or their parents had been living in the state before 25 March 1971. Only those who could prove this would be included in the National Register of Citizens (NRC). Others stood to lose their citizenship.

Possibly the world's largest citizenship verification drive, the

NRC sparked renewed hostility towards Muslim communities. When the prolonged, traumatic process ended in August 2018, over 31 million people found to their relief that their names had been included in the register, but 1.9 million people—about 6.09 per cent of Assam's population—had been left out.

Contrary to the anti-Muslim hysteria that had been whipped up, a smaller fraction of the population in Muslim-majority border districts had been excluded compared to the rest of the state.

Even those currently excluded may eventually be declared Indian citizens. They have the right to challenge their exclusion before specially created tribunals, which have for years adjudicated cases of disputed citizenship. The track record of these tribunals till October 2019 shows that nearly 47 per cent of those who appeared before them—people declared to be foreigners by the state—were upheld as Indian citizens.

The NRC should have settled the debate around illegal immigration and ended the vitriol against Assam's Muslims. But instead of accepting the outcome, Hindutva organizations and the ruling BJP have asked for a recount —a clear and unfortunate attempt to keep the 'population jihad' pot boiling.

CONCLUSION: Assam has seen large scale migration in the colonial era. Since Independence, Assam's population growth rates have not been exceptional. Muslim population is growing because of higher fertility. This can be best controlled by helping them advance, instead of pushing them to the margins.

Chapter 3

FORCED CONVERSIONS

'MLA Goolihatti Shekar Helpless Over His Mother Puttamma's Conversion To Christianity.'

This sensational headline ran as part of a series of 'maha exclusive' stories on the Kannada channel Suvarna News through March 2021. At the heart of the series was a sting operation-style exposé that purported to establish that Puttamma, the seventy-year-old mother of Goolihatti Shekar, a BJP MLA from Karnataka, had been duped by a Christian mafia that was engineering large-scale religious conversions.

The Constitution gives Indians the freedom of religion. They are free to convert to any religion of their choice. But many states have passed laws against forced and fraudulent conversions. Underlying these laws is the assumption that individuals do not convert out of free choice, but are converted by bad actors using force or deceit.

Suvarna News, however, produced no evidence to show Puttamma had been converted either forcibly or fraudulently, other than pointing to the fact that her conversion in 2013 had caught everyone, including her son Shekar, off guard. The coverage closely mirrored the Hindu Right's campaign that casts all conversions to Christianity in a sinister light. A Bangalore-based media watchdog shot off a complaint to the channel, describing its coverage as 'false, unsubstantiated and carefully edited content to construct a false and negative perception about Christians'.

Yet, seven months after the story was aired, it exploded with renewed virality—this time, in the Karnataka assembly. The MLA himself brought up his mother's conversion in an emotionally charged speech in which he claimed 15,000 to 20,000 people had converted to Christianity in his constituency after being 'brainwashed' in the church.

The speech set off shockwaves across Karnataka. Just seven days later, Karnataka chief minister Basavaraj Bommai told reporters: 'Forceful conversions have become rampant. I have directed the district administrations to not allow any religious conversion through inducement or by force as they are illegal.' He also announced the state government's plan to introduce a law to ban forced conversions.

Karnataka's Christian community made frantic appeals to the state government to abort the plan, arguing there was no basis for the claim of rampant forced conversion, and that the law would only embolden vigilantes and fuel anti-Christian bigotry.

The state government claimed the law was not targeted at Christians per se but at forced conversions by all religious groups. But its actions suggested otherwise.

A series of official directives were issued calling for the inspection of churches and Christian prayer halls. No similar directives were passed for any other religious group.

Among the government's actions singling out Christians during this period was a survey conducted in October 2021 in two villages in Chitradurga, part of Goolihatti Shekar's home turf, Hosadurga.

The survey was conducted by the tahsildar, or the local revenue official, on the orders of the district collector. It was ostensibly sparked by a letter written by some residents of Maruti Nagar, a village in Hosadurga taluk, alleging that their village had seen large-scale forced conversions. The letter listed the names of thirty-six people who had been coerced or lured into converting to Christianity, while adding that there were many more such converts in the village.

A day after they received the letter, in a show of surprising alacrity, officials visited Maruti Nagar. They went to the homes of five families to investigate if they had been pressured or lured into converting to Christianity.

Forty-seven-year-old Manjamma was among those surveyed. We met her in July 2022. She recapped to us what she had told the officials: that she had first visited a nearby church over ten years ago, after her husband, Murali, had fallen ill. She had heard from others that praying in the church had helped them recover from illness. She went in the hope that her husband, too, would get better.

'Nobody came to us,' she said. 'It is because of faith that I went there and started praying.' When she took her husband to the hospital, she recalled, a pastor came and prayed with the family and her husband got better. 'I believe in Jesus because he saved my husband's life.'

Manjamma maintained that she was neither forced, nor lured to convert to Christianity. 'It is truly about a belief system,' she said. 'Whoever wants to pray to Anjaneya'—also known as Hanuman—'can pray to him, whoever wants to pray to Jesus can pray to Jesus. I pray only to Jesus.'

To further illustrate her argument, she said, 'See, if there are two kinds of rice, I can choose which rice I want to eat, no?'

The tahsildar's report, submitted in December 2021, concluded that no one had been converted by force or allurement in the two villages. The report punched substantial holes in MLA Shekar's assertions of widespread forcible conversions in the area. Within days of submitting his report, the tahsildar was transferred without a posting.

The tahsildar's report did not stop the government from

pushing ahead with the anti-conversion bill. As it made its way through the legislative process, a wave of attacks erupted against Christians on the grounds that they were carrying out forcible conversions.

All of it—the legislation, the high-pitched anti-Christian rhetoric, the violence—was triggered by the story of Puttamma's 'forced' conversion. But when we met her in July 2022, she denied she had been converted by force.

She told us that she had started going to the church ten years ago after she was hit by a series of personal tragedies— she lost her older son and her husband in separate accidents, and she believed she had been cursed by black magic that made her fall ill.

'Someone came about five days after my son's death,' she said, recalling events from 2012. 'They asked me to come to that God. My husband took me there. Once I went there, I found peace.'

'No one forced me to go or convert,' she said. 'I converted of my own wish.'

In fact, even when she was interviewed on hidden camera by Suvarna News, she can be heard calmly telling her interviewer that she found solace in the Christian faith after the death of her son. Not once did she say anyone had forced or induced her to convert. Yet, the channel ignored her statement.

Months after it aired the story, the channel sent its reporters to Hosadurga once again—this time, to cover a ghar wapsi or homecoming ceremony that Goolihatti Shekhar had organized to bring back his mother and other Christian converts to the Hindu fold.

Sixty-year-old Gouramma, who converted to Christianity over a decade ago, had participated in the so-called reconversion ceremony. 'We were told we will get ₹5 lakh, but we never got it,' she told us. She quickly clarified that she didn't want the money: 'I told them that even if they come and leave the money in my front yard, I would not touch it.'

So what made her attend the ghar wapsi ceremony? Fear, said Gouramma. 'There was a lot being said on TV at the time. That we can't go to God, Hindus can't go to church, Hindus must be Hindus, etc.,' she explained. 'Some people had also come, locals from around here, who said aren't we Hindus, we must stay with Hindus. They also said my ration card will be cancelled.

'When living in a place, we need to get along with the people there, no?' Gouramma said. 'That is why I went to the temple then. To keep the peace.'

While she was leaving the ghar wapsi ceremony, she was given a picture of a Hindu deity. 'It is not here anymore. I gave it to someone,' Gouramma said.

But at the home of Puttamma, the BJP MLA's mother, we noticed a small pooja room filled with Hindu idols and images. There were no visible Christian symbols anywhere.

'They took me to the temple, and brought me back to Hinduism,' Puttamma said. 'I promised I would never go to church.'

Does that mean she is now a Hindu and does not follow Christianity anymore, we asked.

'Don't ask me whether I am Christian or Hindu,' she said, visibly agitated. 'I don't pray to Jesus now, I only think of him silently.'

◆

Most of the conspiracy theories tackled in this book centre around fears of an Islamic takeover. But if there is one area where India's minuscule Christian population occupies an outsized space in the imagination of the Hindu Right, it is in the realm of religious conversions.

According to the Hindu Right, there has been a long-running Western sponsored Christian plot to alter India's religious demography through devious methods.

These fears may have been understandable in newly independent India, emerging from a bruising encounter with Western colonialism and nervous about its future. But seventy-five years later, what drives this persistent paranoia of a Christian takeover?

In the case of the Karnataka MLA's mother, the claims of a conspiracy did not hold up. Do they hold up elsewhere?

In this chapter, we try to find out, starting with one of the Hindu Right's pet theories—Christianity's violent entry into India.

◆

CLAIM: Large-scale forced conversions are real...because Christianity entered and spread in India through the use of force

It is no one's case that India has not seen large-scale forced conversions to Christianity. They did take place—500 years ago.

In the sixteenth century, when the Portuguese arrived on India's western coast, they used conversions as an instrument to establish their rule in Goa. They destroyed temples, transferred their wealth to Catholic orders, and instituted laws and policies that forced local elites to convert.

As the scholar Ângela Barreto Xavier writes in *Religion and Empire in Portuguese India,* 'The refusal to convert had all kinds of negative consequences entailing economic, social, political and cultural marginalisation. They included impoverishing those who resisted, withholding from them the means for survival and access to resources; disruption of family ties; exclusion from cultural practices…and prohibition from holding traditional offices.' The Portuguese even launched an Inquisition to hunt down those who covertly practised their older faith.

The British, who came two centuries later, had a more chequered record. Christian missions followed in the footsteps of the East India Company, with some of its evangelically-minded officials helping them buy land and even using troops to protect them. However, after the 1857 rebellion by Indian soldiers employed in the British army, triggered by the fear that cartridges had been greased in animal fat, the British Crown took over and decided to keep a distance from Christian evangelism. Still, British rule created conditions favourable for Christian missions to proselytize in India—the association with power did not hurt their cause either. The Christian population of India rose during colonial times, as Figure 3.1 shows.

The Hindutva narrative has latched on to the brutality of the Portuguese and the patronage networks enabled by British rule to bolster their claims that Christianity was a violent colonial imposition. Pointedly missing in this narrative is the complexity of the Christian engagement with India.

Christianity did not enter India through the sword. It first came to the subcontinent nearly 2,000 years ago—not from Europe, but from West Asia. A third-century text, *Acts of Thomas*, recounts the story of how Thomas, one of the twelve apostles of Jesus, travelled to India—albeit reluctantly—to spread his message. On the coast of Malabar, Syrian Christian communities believe they are the custodians of this heritage. Even scholars who dispute the historicity of the story agree that Christianity came to India from the Ancient Church of the East, which thrived in what is modern-day Iraq and Iran. As R. S. Sugirtharajah writes in *The Bible and Asia*, 'The Bible did not arrive with the conquering army of a superior civilization in order to subjugate a weak and barbarous people but came with those on the fringes of society to parts of the world where civilization was thriving. The early harbingers of the good news [the gospel] were a motley crowd of missionaries, merchants, persecuted Christians, and travelers with hardly any political power or ambition to conquer.'

The Hindutva narrative also leaves out the complexities of conversions in the colonial era. Conversion under the Portuguese offered 'an opportunity for the underprivileged', Xavier wrote. Lower-caste communities were the first to convert, sensing an 'opportunity to escape their ascribed social fate'. Under British rule, the first converts to Christianity in nineteenth-century Delhi were largely from Dalit groups like the Chamars. In Chotanagpur, in present-day Jharkhand, thousands of Adivasis converted to Christianity and felt empowered to rebel against oppressive landlords.

CONCLUSION: Christianity arrived in India 2,000 years ago—not through conquest. It spread in the colonial era but forced conversions were almost entirely confined to sixteenth-century Goa.

◆

CLAIM: Large-scale forced conversions are real...because census data doesn't count crypto-Christians

When it comes to forced conversions, the Hindu Right is obsessed with India's colonial past. There is a reason for this— it does not have strong data to make the same argument for Independent India.

Christians made up 2.35 per cent of India's population in 1951, when the first census was conducted after Independence.

Since then, the Christian population share has remained at that level. The last census, conducted in 2011, actually showed a marginal dip to 2.3 per cent.

Just this data ought to be enough to debunk the myth of large-scale forced conversions to Christianity in contemporary India.

But Hindu supremacists argue that census numbers don't capture the real picture on the ground because many converts to Christianity conceal their status from the authorities.

'There is something like crypto-Christians,' Alok Kumar of the VHP told us. 'They convert, [but] they don't declare. They live as a Christian, [but] they retain their Hindu names.' He put this down to the fact that 'when a Scheduled Caste converts to Christianity, he loses reservation benefits.'

This is true. India reserves seats in government jobs, public education, and legislatures for Dalit communities listed as Scheduled Castes and Adivasi groups listed as Scheduled Tribes. But conversion to Christianity and Islam leads to a loss of Scheduled Caste status. Dalit converts can no longer access these quotas. While a change in religion does not automatically bar Adivasis from benefiting from affirmative action policies for Scheduled Tribes, many have experienced legal challenges.

Hindutva groups use this fact to bolster their theory of conversion through inducement. According to them, the poor convert to Christianity because missionaries lure them with money, food, medicines, and educational opportunities. The converts choose not to reveal the change in their religious status because they fear losing vital government benefits.

Figure 3.1

India's Christian population rose during colonial times...

Population share, in percentage

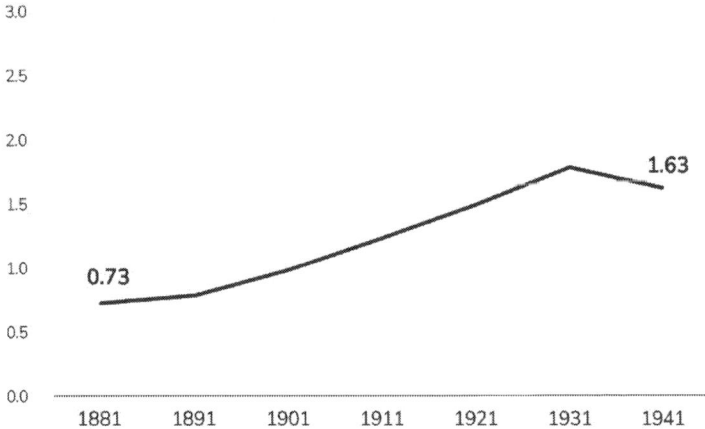

...but has stabilized at less than three percent since then

Population share, in percentage

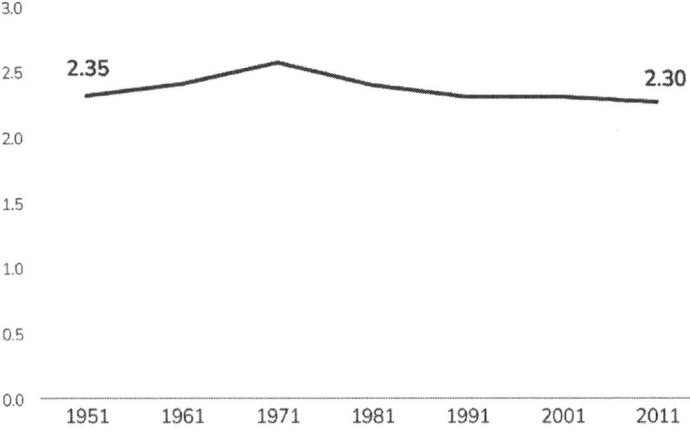

Source: Census of India

We investigated these claims in Karnataka. We interviewed eight people in Maruti Nagar, one of the two villages in Chitradurga district that had been surveyed by the tahsildar after controversy broke out over the conversion of Puttamma, the MLA's mother, in 2021. All eight said they regularly attended church of their own accord—no one had forced or lured them into following Christianity. But at least six of the eight denied they had 'converted', even though most of them had been baptized. What explains this?

We spoke at length with an elderly couple, Savitri and Vishnu, both in their sixties. About fifteen years ago, illness in the family—and the search for a cure—led to their first brush with Christianity.

Those years, they used to travel to Kerala to sell clay jars. 'When we were in Kerala, we used to see churches everywhere,' Savitri said. 'At first, I would get scared seeing Jesus crucified. Then one day, my oldest daughter fell ill, and we took her to the Mission Hospital in Thrissur. It is there that we got enlightenment—Jesus saved her.'

The couple started going to churches regularly. Later, certain people associated with the church came to them and told them 'how to pray'. 'They never forced us. They would just speak to us about the gospel,' Savitri said.

The only time they were offered material incentives to change their faith was when their relatives offered them ₹5 lakh and a car—to return to the Hindu fold. 'They even said they would build us a house,' Savitri said. 'But we just want God.'

Most people in the family now follow Christianity, including three of Vishnu and Savitri's five children, and Vishnu's brother, fifty-year-old Ganesh and his wife, forty-seven-year-old Lakshmi, who live nearby.

Lakshmi said that she had started going to church about twenty years ago in Kerala. 'I used to go to prayers there. But

I hadn't really started following Jesus.' The turning point came when her husband, Ganesh, gave up alcohol under the church's influence. 'We were the leaders of the drunkards. We would get drunk and create a ruckus,' Ganesh recalled, with a smile. 'Then Lakshmi took me to church. First, I had started going, saying, 'I will go only if you buy me booze.' Eventually, as he became more involved with the church, he gave up drinking.

The family got baptised about twelve to thirteen years ago—barring Vishnu, who is still struggling to give up alcohol. Yet, they do not think of themselves as having converted to Christianity. Conversion, for them, means a change in legal status, not a change in faith. 'We have not converted. It is our old caste itself that is mentioned in our Aadhaar,' Lakshmi said.

As members of a Scheduled Caste group, Lakshmi explained that they were aware that 'the benefits we now get from the government as SC, all that will stop if we convert.' Their children have government jobs, which will be jeopardized if they declare they are Christians.

This awareness exists even among missionaries, sociologist Sarbeswar Sahoo points out in his study of religious conversions among Bhil Adivasis in southern Rajasthan. 'The missionaries have distinguished between "believers or followers" and "converts",' he writes. 'Followers are those who believe in Ishu Masih (Jesus Christ), perform prayers and try to bring about changes in their lives… Although the missionaries consider "followers" as Christians, they do not do so in public.' One missionary told him, 'We don't change people's religion; we change their lives…'

For Hindutva groups, this is itself proof of a conspiracy—Christian missionaries are covertly converting people while making them hide their changed status from the government. In reality, however, it isn't Christian groups but the Indian state that is forcing people like Lakshmi and her family to conceal their change in faith. By denying social benefits to Christian converts, it has created a powerful disincentive against public declarations of change in faith.

In recent decades, Dalit Christians and Dalit Muslims have mobilized to demand Scheduled Caste status—a demand which, if granted, would considerably reduce the pressure felt by converts to conceal their changed religious identity.

But the official response to these demands has ranged from indecision to outright resistance. In 2022, the Modi government told the Supreme Court that it rejected a 2007 report recommending Scheduled Caste status to religious minorities. The report, authored by the Justice Ranganath Mishra Commission, had endorsed the view taken by several other government appointed enquiries that despite conversion, Dalit Christians and Muslims have remained saddled with the historical disadvantages of lower caste status. But the government told the Supreme Court that the report was 'myopic' , and announced the setting up of a new commission. The same year, the Sangh Parivar launched a campaign asking for Adivasis who have converted to Christianity and Islam to be denied Scheduled Tribes status and benefits. Several BJP leaders have echoed this view, creating more reasons for Adivasi converts to continue to identify as Hindus.

Scholars have long emphasized that far from being coerced or induced by material goals, conversions to Christianity in India come at a high cost. Sahoo's fieldwork revealed that 'tribals do not find material incentives (which are temporary) significant enough for them to trade in their religion. Additionally, the stigma attached to religious conversion, excommunication of the converts from the community and the loss of traditional identity make conversions too costly for a tribal.'

'If material incentives do not provide a compelling explanation for tribal conversion, what motivates them to take such a big risk?' Sahoo asks. One reason, he points out, is the high burden of illness among Adivasis, and the lack of accessible healthcare. 'Disenchanted by the inaccessible and expensive modern medical system and the exploitative bhopa practices'—bhopa is a traditional healer—'many tribal women visit the church as a last resort,' he writes. They find the church 'welcoming and humane' where 'patients are cared for with love and compassion', without any cost. If they feel better, Adivasi women begin to regularly engage with the church, and gradually introduce the men in their family to it. The church is often able to persuade the men to give up alcohol, which in turns raises the income of the family, improves gender relations, and puts the family on the path of greater prosperity.

The scholars R. S. Shah and T. S. Shah reported similar findings for conversions among Dalit women in the slums of Bengaluru. They said they had experienced social and economic well-being and even acquired a stronger sense of personal identity after they began to attend church services.

What is interesting is that like the Bhil Adivasis of southern Rajasthan, the Dalit women of Bengaluru too had adopted Pentecostal Christianity. Pentecostalism, the fastest growing denomination within Christianity worldwide, differs from other Christian orders in its emphasis on the Holy Spirit. 'They believe...that the Spirit can enter ordinary mortals and give them extraordinary powers,' an article noted. The belief in spirit worship and miracle healing might sit uneasily with other mainline denominations of Christianity, like the Catholic and Protestant orders, but by tapping into 'a deep substratum of primal spirituality', it is able to draw wide support among Indian communities. As Sahoo points out, Pentecostalism 'fits well with the indigenous tribal cosmology and belief system'.

What this likely means is that spiritual belief systems, not just material incentives, are driving conversions to Christianity in India today.

In fact, old and new belief systems often coexist. In 2015, we travelled to a wind-swept settlement in Madhya Pradesh's Khandwa district, where Hindutva activists had disrupted a Christmas feast, alleging Christian pastors were forcibly converting members of a nomadic tribe by gifting them saris. The police went on to arrest ten people, even though the villagers insisted—and photographs clearly showed—that the gifts were given by them to honour their guests. Baffled by the sudden interest in their lives, a daily wage worker leading a hardscrabble existence wondered what all the fuss was about. Referring to Jesus Christ as Prabhu, he told us, 'In our Hindu religion, there are 33 crore gods. Prabhu is one of them only.'

CONCLUSION: Concealment of conversion does not amount to evidence of forced or induced conversion. Rather, it appears to reflect its high cost: not only do converts stand to lose access to reservation benefits, they face stigma, harassment and, increasingly, violence.

◆

CLAIM: Large-scale forced conversions are real...because look at the popular backlash

Every time the Hindu Right intensifies rhetoric against conversions, it inevitably sparks anti-Christian violence. Ask them about it, and the answer goes something like this: yes, violence is avoidable, but if Christians push ahead with forced conversions, there is bound to be a public backlash.

The argument doesn't hold if you look at the most recent episode of large-scale violence against Christians in India.

It took place in Bastar, the Adivasi region of Chhattisgarh.

One morning in December 2022, Christian believers in sixteen villages woke up to copycat attacks—violent mobs ransacked their homes, beat them up, and forced nearly 500 people to flee for their life and safety. Both the attackers and the victims were Adivasis, often from the same village.

Yet, this wasn't a simple case of 'public backlash' against 'forced conversions'.

For one, in conversations with reporters, the believers said they had voluntarily adopted the Christian faith several years ago. The change in faith had caused some friction with their neighbours, especially at the time of village festivals. Although the churchgoers continued to make donations to the common festivities, they declined to accept their share of the food offerings, seen as an insult to the local deities.

But the social tensions did not boil over into violence until a Hindutva organization, the Janjati Suraksha Manch, decided to provoke it. Spearheaded by a former legislator of the BJP, Bhojraj Nag, the Manch held rallies in Bastar through 2022 demanding that those converting to Christianity and Islam be deprived of reservations and other benefits by denying them Scheduled Tribe status.

The December violence erupted not far from Nag's constituency. He justified the violence, arguing not just against the use of force and fraud in religious conversions, but against conversions themselves. 'Let those converting officially declare the change in religion as per law,' he said in an interview. 'They cannot take the benefits of Adivasis and refuse to follow the tradition.'

Just a year earlier, Hindutva groups had aggressively mobilized in another Adivasi belt, the district of Jhabua in Madhya Pradesh, around the same time the BJP government in the state had amended its anti-conversion law. Protest rallies by the VHP demanding the closure of churches for allegedly forcibly converting Adivasis to Christianity began to morph into mob attacks on prayer meetings.

The administration backed the VHP and served notices to pastors, priests, and lay Christians, asking them to furnish information to disprove forced conversions. After six pastors challenged the notices, the Indore High Court stayed them. A day later, Hindutva protestors marched up to the house-cum-prayer hall of one of the pastors who had petitioned the court. The police followed in their footsteps—not to protect the pastor, but to arrest him.

The police's First Information Report cited a complaint by a temple priest, who had ostensibly accused the pastor of trying to forcibly convert him. But when a reporter interviewed the priest, he denied having made such a statement. This fact alone should have undermined the police case against the pastor—according to Madhya Pradesh's amended anti-conversion law, only the person who had been forcibly converted could register a complaint under it.

But there was more. The temple priest told the reporter that the police had summoned him to the police station *after* they had taken the pastor into custody. Essentially, the complaint—and the FIR—were created as a post-facto justification for Hindutva violence.

Organized attacks on Christians by the Hindu Right shown as spontaneous 'public backlash', with the police siding with the mob—similar patterns can also be seen in Karnataka.

In September 2021, as the Karnataka assembly debated an anti-conversion bill, attacks erupted against the state's Christian community. Based on media reports, we counted ten such attacks in four months till the end of the year. Prayer halls and churches were attacked, worshippers beaten up and bullied. In one instance, video footage showed assailants chanting Hindu devotional songs inside a Christian prayer hall.

Almost all the acts of aggression had an organized dimension to them—they were led by Hindutva outfits like the Bajrang Dal and VHP. In several instances, the police went on to file cases against the Christians, citing complaints of forced conversions. However, only in one instance did media reports reference a prior complaint against a pastor.

Strikingly, in two instances, viral videos showed the Christian congregation under attack from Hindutva mobs vehemently rebutting the claim of forcible conversion. For instance, in November 2021, as a Hindutva mob barged into a prayer hall in Hassan, a video of the incident shows women churchgoers confronting the mob. 'What proof do you have of forced conversion?' the women asked. 'We came to the church voluntarily. No one forced us.'

The Hindu Right's hand in anti-Christian violence in recent years is hardly surprising. All major episodes of large-scale violence against Christians in the past three decades have been preceded by mobilization by Hindutva groups that portrayed an increase in Christian population as evidence of forced and fraudulent conversions, even though independent investigations found no evidence for that.

Take, for instance, the ten days of violence that began on Christmas day in December 1998 in the Adivasi-dominated Dangs district of Gujarat. As a human rights organization recorded, 'over twenty churches were burned or destroyed, and scores of individuals were physically assaulted, in some cases tied and beaten up and robbed of their belongings while angry mobs invaded and damaged their homes.'

The provocation appears to have been a year-long, highly vitriolic campaign by Hindutva groups. They distributed pamphlets labelling Christian evangelists as devils and asking Hindus to teach 'these people a lesson'. This, in turn, seemed to be a reaction to the district's changing demography: between

1981-1991, Dangs had seen a four-fold jump in its Christian population from 1.33 per cent of the population to 5.43 per cent. However, this didn't automatically imply the conversions were taking place by force or deceit. As a social worker told the human rights researchers: 'People go to Christianity because they believe they can be cured of disease. They give up drinking and other habits [and thereby] improve their financial position and their domestic relations. They also convert for literacy and education services.' In fact, the allegation of forced conversion was ruled out by both the National Commission of Minorities and an inquiry done by scholars and activists.

A decade later, Kandhamal district of Odisha would see India's worst ever violence against Christians—over 50 people died, scores of women including nuns were raped, 6,000 homes and 300 churches were destroyed. Here, too, groups like the VHP projected the violence as a reaction to forced conversions, ignoring the complex social fault line in the region between the tribal Kandha and the Dalit Pana communities.

Put simply, the Panas were asking for inclusion in the Scheduled Tribes list, sparking resentment among the Kandhas. Over the period of half a century, most Panas had converted to Christianity, while Kandhas had grown Hinduized. A Hindu evangelist working among them, Swami Lakshmanananda Saraswati of the VHP, further stoked the conflict by circulating an exaggerated account of a road skirmish involving him and the Panas. This sparked the first wave of anti-Christian attacks in December 2007. Eight months later, Saraswati was shot dead in his ashram—Maoist insurgents took responsibility for the killing. But it fuelled another, even more deadly, wave of violence against Christians.

HINDU JAGRAN MANCH

Conversion activity by Christian Priests is the most dangerous burning problem at present in Dangs district. Innocent and illiterate tribals are converted through cheating, alluring by offering temptations and other deceiving activities, under the pretext of services, these devils are taking advantage of tribal society and exploit them. In the world, wherever these Christian priests have looted its people and have made them helpless. Lie and deceit are their religion.

Christian priests teach to steal and to tell lies in the name of religion, converted christians today after being concerted write Hindu in their certificate and proof evidences. They condemn Hindu religion and write Hindu to take advantage in Government Programmes.

Hindus, awake and struggle, continuous with these robbers who snatch away your rights by telling lies and teach these people a lesson.

A mammoth rally will be taken out on Monday, 29/06/98 at 11.00 am from Patilwada-Ahwa and will submit memorandum to the Collector.

You are requested to awake for your rights and to join this really in a large number.

Yours,
Co-ordinator
Rameshbhal Chaudhari (Dron)
Hindu Jagran Manch -Dang District

Violence in Gujarat   43

*A pamphlet distributed by the Hindu right wing outfit Hindu Jagran
Manch labelling Christian missionaries as devils,
asking Hindus to teach 'these people a lesson'.*

Ignoring this complex local context, national leaders of the RSS and BJP went on to project the Odisha violence as evidence of the extent of popular anger in India over forced conversions to Christianity. But on the ground, an independent fact-finding inquiry by scholars and lawyers found evidence to the contrary: in the aftermath of the violence, Christians were being forced to convert to Hinduism after 'being chased and herded in groups into Hindu temples and forced to undergo "reconversion" ceremonies with their heads tonsured.' The inquiry report noted: 'They were made to drink cow-dung water as a mark of 'purification' and some of them forced to burn Bibles or damage churches to prove that they had forsaken the Christian faith.'

CONCLUSION: In none of the major instances of violence against Christians in India is there evidence of forcible conversions. Or of a popular backlash. Almost all the attacks appear to be the handiwork of mainstream and fringe Hindutva groups.

◆

CLAIM: Large-scale forced conversions are real...because even non-BJP states are passing anti-conversion laws

Attacks on Christians have often paralleled the passage of anti-conversion laws. Christian groups and legal commentators have for long held that the passage of these laws creates a climate of anti-Christian hate. They say the laws reflect the Hindu Right's default hostility towards religious minorities.

The Hindu Right denies this. It says the laws reflect genuine fears that aren't limited to Hindutva circles.

This is partially true. Debates over conversion animated the Constituent Assembly, tasked with drafting the Constitution. Records of the proceedings capture anxieties across the political spectrum. On 1 May 1947, Sardar Vallabhbhai Patel, who went on to become India's first home minister, moved a clause to insert a ban on forced conversions into the article that guaranteed Freedom of Religion to Indians. He later withdrew the clause, saying conversion by force was already banned under the existing law. '…it is admitted that in the law of the land forcible conversion is illegal. We have even stopped forcible education and, we do not for a moment suggest that forcible conversion of one by another from one religion to another will be recognised,' Patel said.

Members also hotly argued over whether the right to 'propagate' religion, seen as enabling conversions, should be included in the Freedom of Religion Article. 'In the present context what can this word "propagation"... mean? It can only mean paving the way for the complete annihilation of Hindu culture, the Hindu way of life and manners,' said Loknath Misra, a Congressman, later to join the centre-right Swatantra Party.

Eventually, with the backing of a majority of members, the term propagate was retained in Article 25. The final wording read as follows: 'all persons are equally entitled to freedom of conscience and the right freely to profess, practise and propagate religion.' The wording allowed conversions by inference, but stopped short of saying so explicitly in deference to the divided views on the subject. This semantic ambiguity would haunt the conversion question for years to come—did the term 'propagation' in Article 25 mean simply a right to publicize one's religion, or also a right to convert another person to it?

In the aftermath of Independence, the first attempt to pass an anti-conversion law was made by a Congress parliamentarian who moved a private bill in 1954. It failed to muster support. But momentum for a law was building up in some states. In 1954, the Jan Sangh, the BJP's precursor, launched an 'Anti Foreign Missionary Week' in Madhya Pradesh, with weeklong protests against conversions. The Congress-run state government set up a panel under a retired judge Bhawani Shankar Niyogi to inquire into the activities of Christian missionaries.

Those who testified before the committee, as Chad Bauman, Professor of Religion at Butler University, writes in his analysis of the Niyogi Report, were mostly 'upper-caste Hindus who naturally (and correctly) perceived, in the conversion of adivasis and lower-caste Hindus to Christianity, the decline of their power and influence'. They raised the possibility of Christian missionary activity preparing 'the ground for a separate independent State on the lines of Pakistan'. In particular, they feared that the nascent Jharkhand movement would result in the creation of a Christian-dominated state that would eat into parts of Madhya Pradesh. It was, Bauman concludes, 'the manifestation of understandable postcolonial anxieties about the very survival and coherence of the Indian nation.'

The most consequential portion of the Niyogi Report lay in its 'recommendations' section, where it outlined—in a breathless passage—the kind of conversion activity the state should ban: 'any attempt by force or fraud or threats or illicit means or grants of financial or other aid, or by fraudulent means or promises, or by moral and material assistance, or by taking advantage of a person's inexperience or confidence, or by exploiting any person's necessity, spiritual (mental) weakness or thoughtlessness, or in general, any attempt or effort (whether successful or not), directly or indirectly to penetrate into the religious conscience of persons (whether of age or underage) of another faith, for the purpose of consciously altering their religious conscience or faith, so as to agree with the ideas or convictions of the proselytizing party should be absolutely prohibited'.

This language, which can have the effect of banning virtually any type of conversion activity, has seeped into every anti-conversion law introduced since.

Among the first states to use the Niyogi blueprint to pass anti-conversion laws in the late sixties were Odisha and Madhya Pradesh.

The laws immediately sparked legal challenges, ending up in the Supreme Court. The petitioners argued that the legislation was so sweeping and arbitrary in nature that it clamped down on the freedom of any religious group to propagate its religion and gain new adherents. However, an early chance to shut the judicial door on discriminatory lawmaking was lost. In the landmark Stanislaus verdict (1977), the court upheld the Odisha and Madhya Pradesh laws, ruling that while propagation is a fundamental right, conversion is not. The court defined propagation in strictly dictionary terms—granting the right to 'transmit or spread one's religion by an exposition of its tenets', but not 'a right to convert another person to one's own religion'. The great Constitutional jurist H. M. Seervai found the Stanislaus verdict 'clearly wrong' and 'productive of the greatest public mischief.' Of what use is propagation if one cannot advocate conversion, Seervai asked. 'Successful propagation of religion would result in conversion,' Seervai wrote, asking for Stanislaus to be struck down.

The Stanislaus verdict remained. In the ensuing decades, eight more states passed anti-conversion laws, bringing the total count to eleven. Seven of the laws were passed by BJP governments.

While it is true that the initial impulse to clamp down on conversions came from outside the Sangh Parivar, it is now almost entirely a BJP obsession.

We examined all eleven laws and found striking similarities. Almost all are called Freedom of Religion Laws, to suggest free choice, while they actually curb freedoms. One way they do this is by using vaguely defined terms like 'force', 'allurement', and 'fraud'.

Most anti-conversion laws have been passed by BJP governments

- ■ BJP
- ■ Others
- ▨ Both

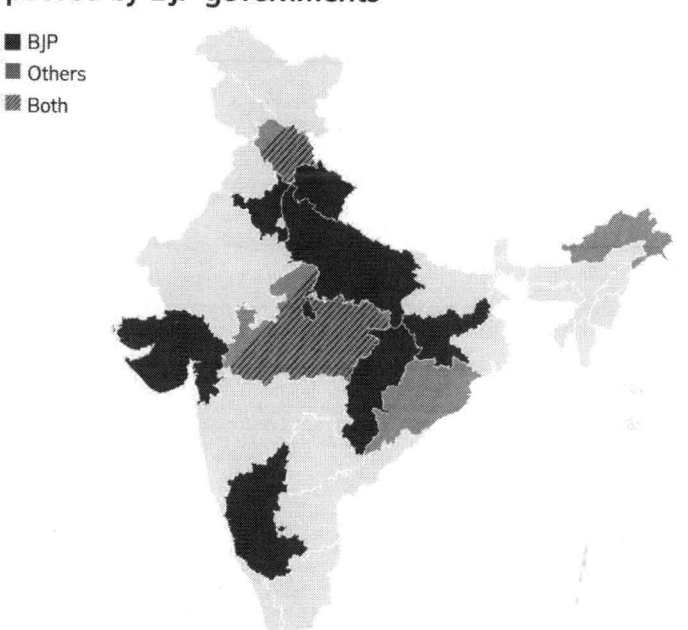

Year	State	Party	Year	State	Party
1967	Odisha	Swatantra Party	2017	Jharkhand	BJP
1968	Madhya Pradesh*	Samyukta Vidhayak Dal	2018	Uttarakhand	BJP
1978	Arunachal Pradesh	Janata Party	2019	Himachal Pradesh	BJP
2003	Gujarat	BJP	2021	Uttar Pradesh	BJP
2006	Himachal Pradesh**	Congress		Madhya Pradesh	BJP
	Chhattisgarh	BJP	2022	Karnataka	BJP
				Haryana	BJP

*   Madhya Pradesh's 1968 law was replaced by a new law in 2021.
** Himachal Pradesh's 2006 law was repealed and later replaced by a new law in 2019.

This map has been prepared in adherence to the 'Guidelines for acquiring and producing Geospatial Data and Geospatial Data Services including Maps' published vide DST ENo. SM/25/02/2020 (Part-I) dated 15th February, 2021.

FORCE

In the anti-conversion laws of eight states, the term force includes 'threats of divine displeasure'. As Shoaib Daniyal points out in *Scroll*, 'farcically, if a missionary informs a person that only Christians are allowed entry into heaven—a core part of the faith—-that could also be construed as "force".'

FRAUD

The same vagueness applies to conversion through 'fraud' or 'fraudulent' means. Daniyal argues 'theoretically, almost any religious tenet not matching scientific fact could be fraud. So, a person preaching that "Adam was the first man on earth" could be committing fraud since there is no way to prove that in the material world.'

ALLUREMENT

The terms 'inducement' or 'allurement' include the sweeping categories of 'divine pleasure', 'blessings' and the promise of a 'better lifestyle'. In other words, virtually anything a preacher may mention in the course of proselytising as attractive qualities of their faith could be construed as illegal.

All laws give inordinate powers to government officials to adjudicate the legality of conversions. In at least four states—Uttarakhand, Himachal Pradesh, Uttar Pradesh, and Jharkhand—the guidelines say that the district magistrate 'shall get an inquiry conducted' into the conversion through the police, effectively treating conversions as a criminal act.

Almost all states require advance notice to be given to district officials by those wishing to convert, ranging from fifteen to sixty days, which, as we have seen in the 'love jihad' chapter, heightens the risk of harassment for those attempting to convert. In nearly half the states, the burden of proof lies on the accused—if you are accused of forced conversions, your accuser doesn't have to furnish evidence against you, rather you must disprove the allegations.

Finally, at least five laws exempt reconversions made to a person's 'immediate previous religion', or 'ancestors' original religion'—mirroring the Hindutva concept of ghar wapsi.

In a 2012 ruling, the Himachal Pradesh High Court struck down the reconversion provision in the state's 2006 anti-conversion law. It also ruled against the provision requiring thirty days public notice. 'A person not only has a right of conscience, the right of belief, the right to change his belief, but also has the right to keep his beliefs secret,' the court ruled.

The 2006 law was repealed. The BJP came to power in the state and replaced it with a new law in 2019, which included the provisions set aside by the high court.

States are going out of their way not just to keep anti-conversion laws on the statute books, but also to make them more stringent. What is the evidence guiding these legislations?

When we put this question to Karnataka chief minister Bommai in August 2022, eight months after the state passed an anti-conversion law, he was not able to provide concrete answers. 'I will give you names of places, please send your cameras there, talk to the poor who have converted, then the truth will come out,' he said. 'My MLA's mother was converted forcibly in Chitradurga by alluring her,' he added, referring to the episode that we have already debunked.

To dig deeper, we filed Right to Information requests with the union Home Ministry and the states that had passed anti-conversion laws, asking for details of cases registered under the laws.

The centre did not respond to our RTIs. Most states pushed them down to the district level, where our questions were brushed aside with officialese. Only four states—Uttar Pradesh, Haryana, Jharkhand, and Arunachal Pradesh—replied with information regarding cases.

The responses from Uttar Pradesh and Haryana are summarized in chapter 1, on 'love jihad', since the anti-conversion laws of those states emerged as an outcome of their political leadership drumming up the need for a law against 'love jihad'.

In Arunachal Pradesh, which has one of the oldest anti-conversion laws, dating back to 1978, as many as nineteen of the twenty-six districts said no cases had been registered under the law. Only two districts reported a case each. The police of East Siang district said a case was registered in 2003, involving an individual who converted from the indigenous religion Donyi-Poloism to Christianity. A reply from East Kameng district mentioned one case of conversion from 2020, but provided no further details.

In Jharkhand, the responses boiled down to a grand total of nine cases in four districts since 2017. Only two featured accusations of conversion to Christianity—hardly matching the Hindutva assertion of a large-scale Christian plot to alter demography.

One of those cases was filed retrospectively. In August 2022, the police in Gumla district booked fourteen individuals for converting to Christianity without following due process—twelve years ago. The police report itself mentions that one of the accused, Bandhan Oraon, said they had all willingly converted to Christianity.

CONCLUSION: The mere existence of India's anti-conversion laws does not lend credence to the claims of illegal conversions. When asked for evidence, states that had passed the laws supplied none.

CLAIM: Forcible conversions are real because...a Hindu schoolgirl in Tamil Nadu, under pressure to convert, died by suicide

Our RTIs requests largely drew a blank. Just as we felt the search for credible proof of large-scale forced conversions had hit a wall, a document surfaced in the public domain, which claimed to tabulate precisely that.

This was a petition filed in the Supreme Court in 2022 by Delhi-based advocate and former BJP spokesperson Ashwini Upadhyay, asking the court to direct the centre to pass a national anti-conversion law. To bolster his plea, the petition contained supposed instances of forcible conversion.

Twice, the Delhi High Court had rejected Upadhyay's petitions on the matter, pulling him up for lack of evidence on one occasion. Even the Supreme Court in 2021 threatened to impose costs on him if he pursued the matter further. Yet, in November 2022, the court did a U-turn.

'The issue with respect to the alleged conversion of religion, if it is found to be correct and true, is a very serious issue which may ultimately affect the security of the nation and violate citizens' right to freedom of conscience and right to freely profess, practice and propagate religion,' it said, asking the centre to file its response on how it plans to 'curb such forced conversion'. Such strong language from India's top court merited a closer look at Upadhyay's submissions. His petition began with sweeping generalizations. Some examples:'Not even one district is free of religious conversion by hook or crook', 'mass religious conversions (of) SC-ST is on a steep rise', and 'conversions are primarily rooted in a surge of international conversion campaigns'.

As evidence, he provided a list of fifteen cases, a number hardly commensurate with the allegation of a widespread conspiracy.

Of the fifteen cases, only two featured claims of mass conversions. In both cases, the allegation was that American Christian missions—the Houston-based Central India Christian Mission and the Missouri-based Joyce Meyer Ministries—had separately converted about 21,000 people in India in 2010. In neither case did the petition provide a source of information for the allegations, nor did it explain how these amounted to forcible conversions. In three other cases, Upadhyay did not even bother spelling out basic details: for instance, he claimed a 'boy from a minority community' had concealed his identity while dating a Hindu woman, until it was time for marriage, when he forced her to convert. No name or place was mentioned.

In ten cases, the allegation revolved around students in Christian schools. Two were from Madhya Pradesh, where it was alleged that children had been forcibly converted in schools in Vidisha and Raisen districts, in 2021. In both cases, media reports had punctured holes in the allegations. In the Vidisha case, the media reported that the children were already Christian.

The petition also cited six examples of Hindu students in Christian schools being made to remove their religious markers or being punished for wearing them. For instance, in 2021, a missionary school in Telangana reportedly refused to allow a student wearing a religious necklace to enter the school. In another instance, girl students in a convent school in Bharuch, Gujarat, were allegedly not allowed in class because they had henna on their hands. In none of these examples was any evidence supplied by Upadhyay to show how this amounted to forced conversion.

Upadhyay's petition also referenced a viral video from October 2021, of a student being beaten by a Christian teacher in Tamil Nadu. The petition quoted news reports claiming the beating was punishment because the boy wore a rudraksh, or religious necklace, and sandalwood on his forehead. A fact-check of the video found the teacher was a Hindu man named Subramanian, who thrashed a student for skipping class.

When we interviewed Upadhyay, he brushed aside our questions, saying he has more evidence which he will present in court. 'There are supplementary affidavits and additional documents. You don't have the real version,' he said. When we persisted, Upadhyay walked away from our cameras.

However, one case stood out in Upadhyay's petition. No less than India's federal agency, the Central Bureau of Investigation, was probing it.

Could this be the 'gotcha' moment that proves the Hindu Right's claim of forcible conversion? We travelled to Tamil Nadu to find out.

We went to Thanjavur district, in the south of the state. On 15 January 2022, Lavanya Muruganandam, a Class 12 student at Sacred Heart Convent, had been admitted to a government hospital in Thanjavur city, a week after she attempted to kill herself by drinking pesticide in her school hostel.

In statements to the police and to a local judge, made from her hospital bed, Lavanya blamed Sister Sagaya Mary, the hostel warden, for her suicide bid. Sagaya Mary, she said, made her and the other students perform menial tasks like cleaning the hostel and clearing grass from the common garden. She said a tipping point came on 9 January when the warden scolded her yet again, prompting her to drink the pesticide. Her father, Muruganandam, repeated the same sequence of events to the police. Based on the family's complaint, the police arrested Sagaya Mary on charges of abetting the suicide of a minor.

Until this point, no one—neither Lavanya nor her family—even hinted at forcible conversion, or even conversion per se.

Six days later, Lavanya died. Suddenly, a conversion controversy erupted. The sole basis: a viral video, recorded two days earlier by Muthuvel, a local functionary of the VHP.

The clip begins abruptly, with Lavanya describing an incident from about two years ago, when she said a school official 'asked my parents in front of me "shall I convert your daughter to Christianity and get her education?"'

Was she harassed by the school authorities because she refused to convert, asks Muthuvel.

'Could be,' says Lavanya.

When asked to identify the nun who had made the conversion offer, Lavanya names Raquel Mary, who had served as the warden of the school hostel in 2019.

On the basis of this 44-second clip—of a tentative-sounding Lavanya responding to leading questions from a VHP man—the Hindutva ecosystem built a sustained, high-decibel campaign. Here was clinching proof, not just of forced conversion, they said, but of how pressure to convert to Christianity was so intense that it was pushing Hindus to take their own lives.

Decades of medical research has underscored that suicide is a complex phenomenon which cannot be reduced to a single factor. Lavanya's biological mother, Kanimozhi, had committed suicide in 2013. The same year, her father married Saranya, Lavanya's stepmother. As we shall see shortly, multiple accounts described Lavanya as a brilliant but withdrawn child, unhappy with her home life.

Moreover, the police found Muthuvel had recorded more than one video of Lavanya, but chose to release only the clip which mentions the conversion offer. In another recording—not released by him, but which surfaced subsequently—Lavanya makes no mention of conversion. In this 2 minute 44 second long clip she tells Muthuvel what she told the police—that she attempted to take her life because of harassment by the hostel warden. 'The sister at my boarding school would always ask me to do mathematics. She would never listen even if I told her that I couldn't understand the concepts because I joined 'late,' Lavanya says. 'Even if I write it correctly, she would say it is incorrect and make me sit for an hour, to solve just one math problem…. As this continued, I thought that I won't be able to study and therefore I consumed poison.'

Yet, the Hindu Right is clear why Lavanya took her own life—the pressure to convert to Christianity.

In the aftermath of Lavanya's suicide, such posts flooded social media.

The Hindutva narrative found support from Lavanya's father and stepmother. They had made no mention of conversion when Lavanya was alive but a day after the viral video surfaced, they changed tack. In a fresh statement to the police, the father said that some years ago, when he and his wife had visited the school hostel, the warden had told them that Lavanya was 'doing well in her studies'. The warden said 'they would take care of our daughter' and offered to convert her to Christianity. 'Irked over such words, my wife Mrs. Saranya shouted at her in anger.' Yet, he added that they did not take it 'as a serious matter'.

Two days later, they dramatically upped the ante. In fresh statements to a local magistrate, the parents claimed three nuns at the school had tortured Lavanya for refusing to convert to Christianity, pushing her to take her life. They moved the high court to demand the transfer of the case to the CBI—a demand also made by the state unit of the Tamil Nadu BJP. Both the parents and the BJP alleged the local police had acted in a biased manner. The court agreed, ordering the transfer of the case to the CBI.

Nearly a year and half after Lavanya's death, we met her parents at their home in a village in Ariyalur, near Thanjavur. When we asked them about their daughter's suicide, Muruganandam spoke at length about the harassment she had been subjected to. 'Our *papa* (daughter) was made to do all the work at the school'. He did not once mention the school's supposed conversion offer. When we brought it up, Saranya had only a brief answer: 'When we went to pick up Lavanya, one of the sisters told us "We will put her through her studies. We will keep her in our matham (community)". We rejected the offer, saying we know how to raise our child.'

Was the offer made in a forceful manner, we asked.

'No, it just came up as part of the conversation,' said Saranya.

So why did they accuse the school of torturing her to convert?

'We came across that issue after Muthuvel's video became public,' Saranya said.

We asked them how Muthuvel came into the picture. Muruganandam told us when Lavanya was admitted to hospital, he had contacted his cousin, Aiyarappan, who had connections to the BJP. The cousin, he said, brought the VHP man to the hospital.

In their submissions to the court, lawyers for the Sacred Heart convent have vehemently denied attempts to convert Lavanya to Christianity. The school, a 164-year-old institution founded by a Catholic mission based in Puducherry—the Order of the Immaculate Heart of Mary—has always admitted students of all faiths, they said. At the time of the incident, of the 786 students studying in the school, 504 were Hindus.

We interviewed almost a dozen parents of current and former students of the Sacred Heart Convent. Some of them had themselves studied at the school, with the connection to it going back generations.

All of them said they had never come across attempts by the school to pressure students to convert.

Mahalakshmi, forty-eight, graduated from the school in 1988. Three of her sisters—Shakuntala, Subbulakshmi, and Shanti—had also studied at Sacred Heart. Her father worked in the school as a carpenter. Her son, Guhan, is currently in Class 10. Her daughter, Vijayalakshmi, Lavanya's classmate, had never heard her complain of any pressure to convert, Mahalakshmi said.

Vijay Kumar sent all three of his children to Sacred Heart. Manoj, nineteen, recently graduated. Madhumita, seventeen, is currently in Class 12, and Balaji, thirteen, is in Class 8. 'I am a Hindu, but I have learnt discipline and honesty from the Church,' Kumar told us. The school, he said, could never pressure anyone to convert.

Jasima, forty-nine, studied at Sacred Heart till Class 10. Her daughter, Majida Fathima, and son, Fahad, now study there. She laughed off the suggestion of conversion. 'Our children are allowed by the school to fast during Ramzan. Our daughters can wear hijab,' she said.

K. Chandru, twenty-seven, a software engineer with Influx Worldwide, a digital marketing company, graduated from the school in 2013. He said when he saw allegations of forced conversion against the school on the news, he 'immediately knew it was a lie'.

At eighty-three, J. Gurumurthy is a long-time resident of Michaelpatti, the village where the convent is located. He retired after thirty-three years as a teacher in a neighbouring school. Three of his daughters, now in their forties and fifties, studied at Sacred Heart. 'We were shocked when we heard the news' of the suicide, he said. 'The school received a bad name, for no reason.'

We met Sagaya Mary, sixty-three, currently out on bail, in a residence for nuns in Tiruchirappalli, an hour from Thanjavur. She denied bullying Lavanya, or singling her out for menial chores. She had a completely different account of the distress in Lavanya's life: she said the child did not want to go home, and would stay over at the hostel even during school holidays, forming a close bond with her.

In statements to the police, six of Lavanya's classmates have confirmed how unhappy she was at home, particularly because of her strained relations with Saranya. One of them, Yogavi, seventeen, told the police Lavanya had a burn mark on the palm of her hand, which Lavanya told them was inflicted by her stepmother.

Sister Apolin, the principal of Sacred Heart School, told us the stepmother suspected Lavanya had stolen money and had placed burning camphor in the palm of her hand as a test.

The school had treated the burn when it came to their notice.

Even Lavanya's maternal grandaunt, Nithiyananda Saraswati, told the police that she had lodged a complaint with the Tamil Nadu government's child helpline about the burn mark in July 2020.

But Lavanya's father denied the incident. 'No such thing happened,' he said. The parents claimed the school would not allow Lavanya to come home during the holidays, because they were exploiting her for work.

We contacted the VHP's Muthuvel, but he told us he could not come on the record because of the ongoing investigation.

We were directed to R. Sethuraman, the VHP's organizing secretary for southern Tamil Nadu. When we asked him about the multiple anomalies in the Hindu Right's narrative of forced conversion, he claimed ignorance. 'I have not seen all the statements,' he told us.

Running out of answers, he pulled out a bizarre accusation— the Superintendent of Police of Thanjavur, who led the initial investigation into the case, is Christian, he said, which explains why the police went soft on the school.

The Thanjavur superintendent at the time was Ravali Priya. When we contacted her, she was bemused at the VHP leader's allegation. 'I am a devout Hindu,' she told us, laughingly. 'My name means the sound made by the anklets of Lord Krishna'.

CONCLUSION: The claim of attempted forced conversion in the Lavanya case is not backed by credible or conclusive evidence.

Chapter 4

MUSLIM APPEASEMENT

India's most populous state, Uttar Pradesh, is also one of its poorest. Six of every hundred children born in the state die before the age of five—the worst child mortality in the country, worse than even some countries in sub-Saharan Africa. Yet, addressing an election rally in February 2017, Prime Minister Narendra Modi identified 'bhed bhaav'—or discrimination—as Uttar Pradesh's biggest crisis.

A bulk of the state's resources, he said, were being cornered by one family—a barb directed at a political rival, the Samajwadi Party founder, Mulayam Singh Yadav. But Modi didn't stop there. He went on to sweepingly claim: 'And the rest goes to Muslims.'

Modi's speech had built up to a familiar theme in Indian politics: Muslim appeasement, or the idea that certain political parties like the Samajwadi Party cultivate Muslims as a vote bank by giving them preferential treatment.

The BJP had pushed this view for decades, but it was rare for an Indian prime minister to air such a grievance.

'Brothers and sisters, if a village gets a kabristan, it should get a shamshan too,' Modi went on to say.

The accusation that Muslim graveyards had been prioritized over Hindu cremation grounds was based on facts. In 2012, the Samajwadi Party government had launched a scheme to fortify the boundary walls of Muslim graveyards and funeral sites of other religious minorities. After the BJP protested, the government also sanctioned funds for Hindu cremation grounds, albeit on a smaller scale.

Figure 4.1

After its Muslim graveyard scheme caused a furore, UP's Samajwadi Party government also allocated funds for Hindu cremation grounds

Funds allocated, in crore rupees

■ Burial grounds   ■ Cremation grounds

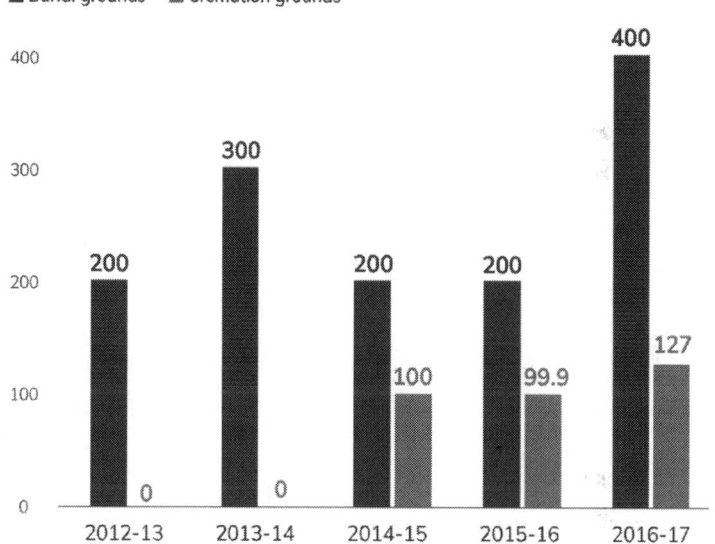

Source: Uttar Pradesh Budgets

But Modi went on to make a puzzling assertion: 'If there is electricity during Ramzan, there should be electricity during Diwali. If there is electricity during Holi, there should be electricity during Eid,' he said.

Modi seemed to be implying that religious discrimination under the Samajwadi Party government extended to electricity distribution. Yogi Adityanath, the BJP leader who went on to become the chief minister of Uttar Pradesh in 2017, spelt it out more clearly. In an election speech in 2019, he claimed that under the Samajwadi Party government electricity was provided during Eid, but was not during Diwali. He claimed that the newly elected BJP government had ended this discriminatory practice.

Was this the case?

We looked up daily electricity reports from the Power System Operation Corporation Limited, a central government agency that monitors electricity supply across India.

The results were startling.

Figure 4.2

Uttar Pradesh's electricity data debunks the BJP's claim that the Samajwadi Party government favoured Eid over Diwali

Maximum electricity demand met in a day, in KW

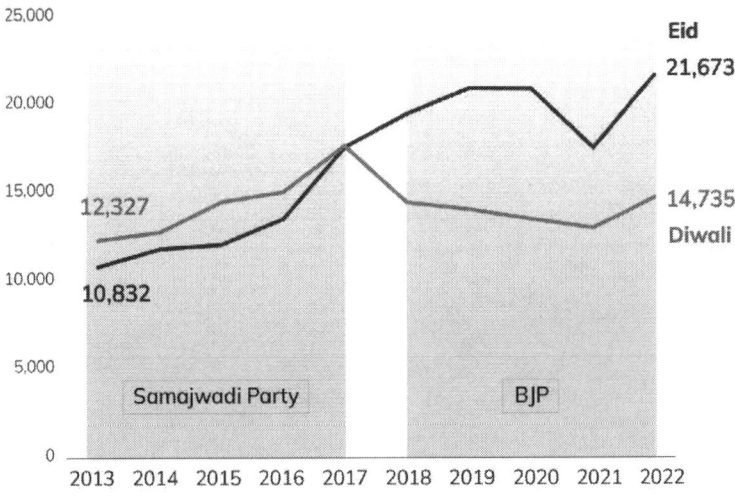

Source: Power System Operation Corporation Limited

Between 2013 and 2017, under the Samajwadi Party, more electricity was supplied in Uttar Pradesh on the day of Diwali than on Eid. Starting 2018, when the BJP came to power, there was a reversal: electricity supplied on Eid outstripped the supply on Diwali.

Does this mean the BJP—and not the Samajwadi Party— was appeasing Muslims? Clearly not. Electricity supply isn't linked to festivals and communities, it reflects larger factors like varying seasonal demand. On average, power supply across India is higher in summer months compared to the rest of the year. During the Samajwadi years, Eid had fallen in the monsoon months of July and August, while in the BJP years, Eid shifted to the much warmer months of May and June.

But facts often take a backseat when it comes to communal politics. The false claim about the Samajwadi Party government supplying more electricity on Eid than on Diwali has now become part of the burgeoning collective memory of Muslim appeasement in India—a theory that casts Muslims as pampered citizens who receive an undue share of state largesse. The reality is starkly different. Muslims are amongst the most underprivileged communities in India, as we shall see shortly.

And yet, nothing has bolstered support for the Hindu Right more than the perception that the Indian state has mollycoddled Muslims at the cost of Hindus. One of the reasons for the theory's longevity (and potency) is that unlike other Hindutva claims, the idea of appeasement is less easy to dismiss outright.

For one, India's Constitution itself has enshrined special protections for minorities. In the aftermath of Partition, the Republic's founders were emphatic about the need to allay minority anxieties, especially the concerns of Muslims who had stayed back in India. To the Hindu Right, this was clear evidence of the nascent Indian state favouring Muslims over Hindus—a contention we explore later in the chapter. Using this premise, the Hindu Right has built a mountain of grievance on a kernel of facts.

Take, for example, Modi's 2017 speech. The kabristan versus shamshan comparison shows the Samajwadi Party government was indeed rolling out Muslim-centric schemes. But what was the amount spent on them that so incensed Modi? The total allocation on the Muslim graveyard scheme between 2012 and 2017 was about 0.1% of the state's budget.

This holds true of most of the examples of Muslim-centric policies that infuriate the Hindu Right. The minuscule amounts assigned to these schemes show them up to be little more than token gestures, nowhere close to the alarmist perception of Muslims draining India's resources.

For instance, the Tamil Nadu government came under criticism for paying a monthly pension to ulemas, or Muslim clerics, of ₹3,000 a month. This is lower than the ₹4,000 per month pension that the state government gives to temple priests. Besides, in 2023-24, the total expenditure on the ulema pension scheme was ₹5.4 crores, 0.001% of Tamil Nadu's total budget.

The success of the appeasement claim lies in exaggerating these stray items of expenditure and linking them with outright falsehoods—as Modi and Adityanath did with their claims about bias in power generation—to create an impression of monumental minority pandering.

Nowhere is this strategy more evident than in the Hindu Right's attacks on a speech by Modi's predecessor, Prime Minister Manmohan Singh.

CLAIM: Appeasement is real because...the prime minister of a Congress-led government gave Muslims the first right to India's resources

In the winter of 2006, Hindutva circles were buzzing with outrage. Prime Minister Manmohan Singh, who headed a Congress-led government, had said the unthinkable—that Muslims deserve the first share of India's resources.

Singh's exact words, delivered during a speech to the National Development Council, are reproduced below:

> We will have to devise innovative plans to ensure that minorities, particularly the Muslim minority, are empowered to share equitably in the fruits of development. They must have the first claim on resources.

The backlash to these comments was so severe that the Prime Minister's Office had to issue a clarification. It said the prime minister was referring to marginalized groups as a whole, not Muslims alone.

To drive home the point, the statement cited the lines that came before Singh's comment on minority empowerment:

> I believe our collective priorities are clear: agriculture, irrigation and water resources, health, education, a critical investment in rural infrastructure, and the essential public investment needs of general infrastructure, along with programs for the upliftment of SC/STs, other backward classes, minorities and women and children.

The squabble over the interpretation of Singh's speech aside, the reality of Muslim backwardness is hardly in doubt.

In November 2006, a month before the prime minister's speech, a committee headed by a retired judge Rajinder Sachar, set up to look into the social and economic status of Muslims, submitted its report to the government.

A social media post from January 2023 criticizes
Manmohan Singh for his 2006 speech.

It reiterated what scholars had long held—that on virtually every social and economic indicator, Muslims were at the bottom of Indian society. The reality holds to the present day.

LIVING STANDARDS

Muslims in rural India spend the least on consumption among all religious groups, according to the last available National Sample Survey data. While Sikhs had the highest average monthly expenditure at ₹2,106, for Hindus, it was ₹1,172, and for Muslims, it was ₹1,133.

LITERACY AND EDUCATION

Illiteracy is the highest among Muslims compared to all religious communities, according to the 2011 Census. Fewer Muslims have studied till Class 10 and Class 12 compared to members of other religious communities. Graduate education among Muslims is less than half the level among Hindus.

SALARIED JOBS

Muslims lag behind on salaried jobs and regular wages. In 2021–22, while 49.50 per cent of urban Hindu workers earned a regular wage or had salaried jobs, only 33.40 per cent of Muslim workers did so, according to the Periodic Labour Force Survey.

BUSINESS

Muslims make up 14.20 per cent of the population but constitute only 2.67 per cent of the senior leadership of the top 500 companies listed on the Bombay Stock Exchange, analysis by the *Economic Times* in 2015 showed.

Figure 4.3

Muslims are at the bottom of the heap when it comes to graduate education

Percentage that has studied till the graduate level or above, by religion

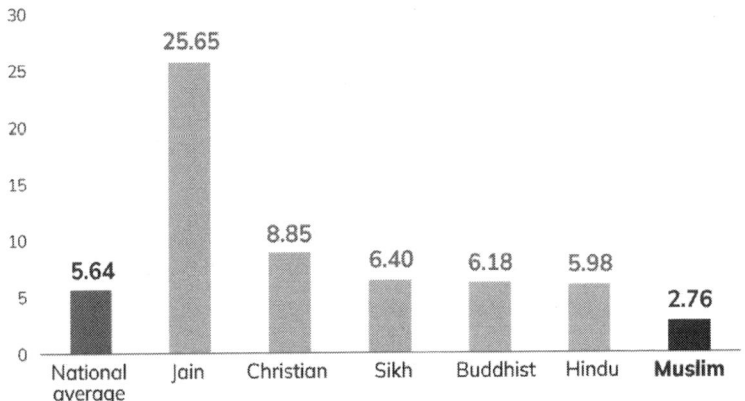

Source: Census of India, 2011

POLICE

Muslim representation in the police force hovered between 3-4 per cent, according to an analysis of the annual reports of the National Crime Records Bureau from 1999 to 2013. From 2014 onwards, the government has stopped compiling data in this category.

Given how severely Muslims lag behind and how poorly they are represented in key areas, there is a strong case for greater targeted support for Muslims, not less.

In reality, resource allocation to religious minorities has been a blip in India's overall welfare spending, even under the Congress.

We looked at the budgetary allocations to the Ministry of Minority Affairs which was set up in 2006 when the Congress-led United Progressive Alliance (UPA) government was in power.

Until 2014, when the UPA was voted out of power, we found the ministry's annual budget ranged between less than 0.1% to just above 0.2% of India's overall budget. Since 2014, when the BJP came to power, this paltry yearly outlay has further reduced, with allocations falling to 0.07% in 2023-24.

Figure 4.4

The allocation to the Ministry of Minority Affairs was minuscule under the UPA, and fell further under the NDA

Allocation as a percentage of the Union budget

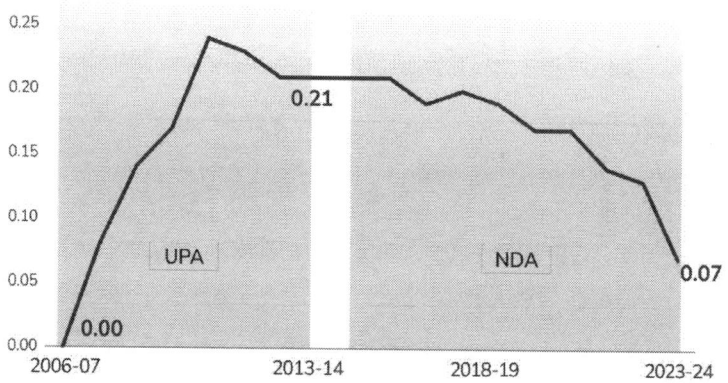

Source: Annual budget documents

To be clear, inadequate funding plagues government schemes for all marginalized groups, not just for Muslims. Welfare measures for Scheduled Castes and Scheduled Tribes, for instance, are chronically underfunded. But the difference is that Muslims have been largely excluded from one of the most powerful tools in the arsenal of the Indian state to counter historic discrimination—affirmative action in the form of reservations in public employment, education, and legislatures. This, despite the fact that most Muslims are converts from communities that carry the historical burden of caste.

Some believe this may explain why, on certain metrics, Muslims even slip below Dalits and Adivasis.

A recent study on intergenerational mobility in India—found that at the 29th percentile of the distribution of parents in the bottom half of Indian society, Muslim sons 'have considerably worse upward mobility today than both Scheduled Castes (38) and Scheduled Tribes (33), a striking finding given that, compared to Muslims, STs tend to live in more rural and remote areas'.

The authors of the study tentatively propose an explanation for this divergence between Muslims and SCs and STs: 'we find suggestive evidence that the basket of affirmative action policies targeted to India's scheduled groups (but not to Muslims) has played a key role in their rising mobility.'

Data from the National Sample Survey conducted in 2017–18 throws up an even more granular picture of how Muslims have now fallen behind Scheduled Castes and Scheduled Tribes. A key metric to gauge the educational levels of a social group is the gross attendance ratio or the total number of children attending school as a proportion of the total number of children from the group. Of every 100 Muslim children, 85 are in school. The corresponding number for SC and ST children is 90 and 87.

Even when it comes to attending college and university, Muslim enrolment numbers have decreased by 8 per cent, while SC and ST enrolment has gone up.

Muslims form 14.20 per cent of India's population. But the All India Survey on Higher Education found only 4.65

per cent of the 41.3 million students enrolled in colleges and universities in 2020–21 were Muslim. In comparison, students from Scheduled Caste groups that form 16.6 per cent of India's population accounted for 14.20 per cent of the enrolment, while students from Scheduled Tribes, that constitute 8.60 per cent of the population, accounted for 5.80 per cent of the enrolment.

Income data also shows Muslims slipping behind. The per capita annual income of Muslims is lower than Dalit Hindus in several states, data from the Indian Human Development Survey of 2004–05 and 2011–12 shows.

As we reported in an earlier chapter, demands that Dalit Muslims (and Dalit Christians) be recognized as Scheduled Castes have been growing. But there is still a long way before this can become a reality. As a halfway measure, some states have included Muslim communities in the list of Other Backward Classes (OBCs). Even these half measures are coming undone. In April 2023, the BJP government in Karnataka scrapped OBC reservation for Muslims, distributing the quota between Hindu communities. Even though the Muslim reservation had been granted on economic grounds, India's home minister praised the move, saying the quotas amounted to minority appeasement and deserved to be done away with.

CONCLUSION: The Hindu Right has it backwards. Far from being pampered by the Congress, Muslims are at the bottom of the heap. If the Congress is guilty of anything, it is of failing to uplift Muslims despite enjoying the longest stint in power.

CLAIM: Appeasement is real because...of the hajj subsidy

Instead of focusing on the monumental evidence of Muslim backwardness, Hindutvavadis are fixated on relatively insignificant items of government expenditure seen to solely benefit Muslims, like the hajj subsidy.

For decades, Hindutva organizations have railed against Indian taxpayer money being spent on subsidizing Muslim pilgrimage to Mecca in Saudi Arabia.

Does the extent of resentment match the actual spending?

Before we answer that question, it is worth noting that the origins of government-sponsored hajj pilgrimages do not lie with the Congress. The practice goes back to India's colonial era. In 1918, Britain used the hajj to shore up its image in the Muslim world by sponsoring the pilgrimage of 2,000 Indian Muslim soldiers in Egypt. In 1932, the British government in India set up Port Haj Committees in Bombay, Calcutta, and Karachi. Governments in post-Independence India continued this practice, first subsiding sea travel and eventually flights to Mecca, sparking decades-long criticism.

The backlash did not come just from the Hindu side. The hajj scheme was denounced by Muslims leaders too.

To explain, the hajj subsidy was not an amount directly given to Muslim pilgrims, instead it was paid by the civil aviation ministry to the airlines that ferried them to Arabia. Since a bilateral agreement between Saudi Arabia and India limited the pool of eligible airlines to the official carriers of the two countries, it gave Air India a virtual monopoly on the route, leading to the accusation that it was charging higher than normal fares for the journey. Air India justified the higher fares on the basis that the planes returned to India nearly empty after dropping the pilgrims, and similarly flew back empty at the end of the pilgrimage season to pick them up.

Muslim leaders pointed out that allowing more airlines to bid for the hajj pilgrimage route would have brought down the cost of the airfare. In one stroke, the need for the subsidy would be eliminated and the Hindu Right deprived of a favourite scapegoat. Others had an even more fundamental disagreement: they said the hajj subsidy was un-Islamic since Islamic law mandated that Muslims pay for the travel out of their own earnings.

In the midst of these debates, the Hindutva campaign against the hajj subsidy gained traction. Prafull Goradia, a former BJP Rajya Sabha MP, petitioned the Supreme Court asking for the hajj subsidy to be abolished, arguing that it violated his fundamental rights under a constitutional clause which prohibits the collection of taxes to promote a particular religion. 'The grievance of the petitioner is that he is a Hindu but he has to pay direct and indirect taxes, part of whose proceeds go for the purpose of the hajj pilgrimage, which is only done by Muslims,' the court said, summarizing Goradia's arguments before rejecting them in its 2011 order. It said: 'In our opinion, if only a relatively small part of any tax collected is utilised for providing some conveniences or facilities or concessions to any religious denomination, that would not be violative of Article 27 of the Constitution.'

The court effectively dismissed the charge that the hajj subsidy was a form of religious discrimination or appeasement. But the next year, another bench of the Supreme Court took the view that the hajj subsidy violated Islamic law. Citing the Quran, it said: '…we have no doubt that a very large majority of Muslims applying to the Haj Committee for going to Haj would not be aware of the economics of their pilgrimage and if all the facts are made known a good many of the pilgrims would not be very comfortable in the knowledge that their Hajj is funded to a substantial extent by the Government.' It asked for the hajj subsidy to be phased out in ten years.

Six years later, in January 2018, the Modi government announced the end of the subsidy, with the grand claim of 'Empowerment without Appeasement'.

So what was the extent of the 'appeasement'? ₹8,674 crore in twenty-five years, or ₹350 crore per year. (See graph below.)

Figure 4.5

The Haj subsidy, 1994-2017

Amount, in crore rupees

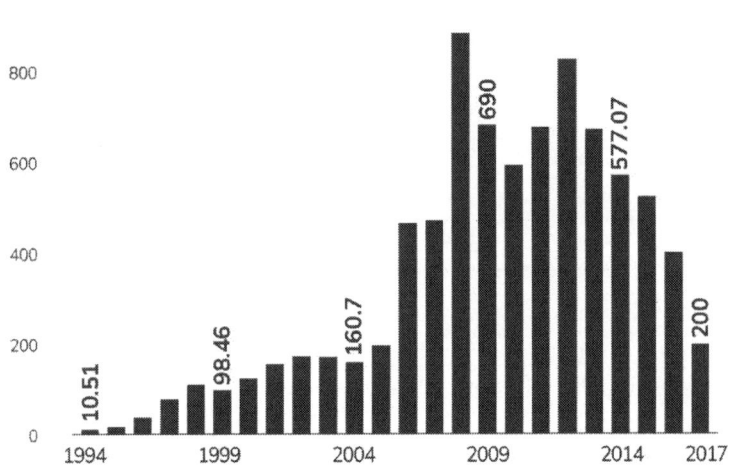

Source: Ministry of Civil Aviation

To put this in perspective, the government budgeted ₹4,236 crore in a single year for the Ardh Kumbh festival, held in Allahabad in 2019.

Every three years, a Kumbh mela is held at one of the four locations—Allahabad, Haridwar, Nashik, Ujjain. In addition, Allahabad hosts an Ardh Kumbh every six years. On each of these events, hundreds of crores of rupees of taxpayer money is spent.

Some may argue that the Kumbh is a mass gathering and the expenditure is towards creating public facilities. But what about the growing state subsidies to Hindu pilgrims? Today, these schemes are so wide-ranging that it is impossible to present an exhaustive summary. Here is a sample:

KAILASH MANSAROVAR

Several states provide financial assistance to pilgrims travelling to the Kailash Mansarovar lake in Chinese-administered Tibet. Rajasthan, for instance, has been offering an assistance of ₹1 lakh since 2011.

STATE PILGRIMAGE SCHEMES

Madhya Pradesh was the first state to launch a chief minister's pilgrimage scheme in September 2012. From ₹59 crore that year, the annual expenditure on the scheme rose to ₹164 crore in 2017–18.

The scheme covered travel to fifteen religious sites—twelve of them Hindu, one Sikh, one Jain. The only site connected to Islam is Ajmer Sharif, the shrine of a Sufi saint revered by non-Muslims too.

Chhattisgarh followed in the footsteps of MP, launching a similar scheme in 2013. Expenditure on the scheme rose to ₹45 crore by 2017–18.

Delhi launched a pilgrimage scheme in 2018. Called the Tirth Yatra Yojana, it features ten routes. Barring one, all are to Hindu religious destinations. In 2023–24, it allocated ₹80 crore for the scheme.

Figure 4.6

Several states give a subsidy to travel to Kailash Mansarovar

Amount per pilgrim, in rupees

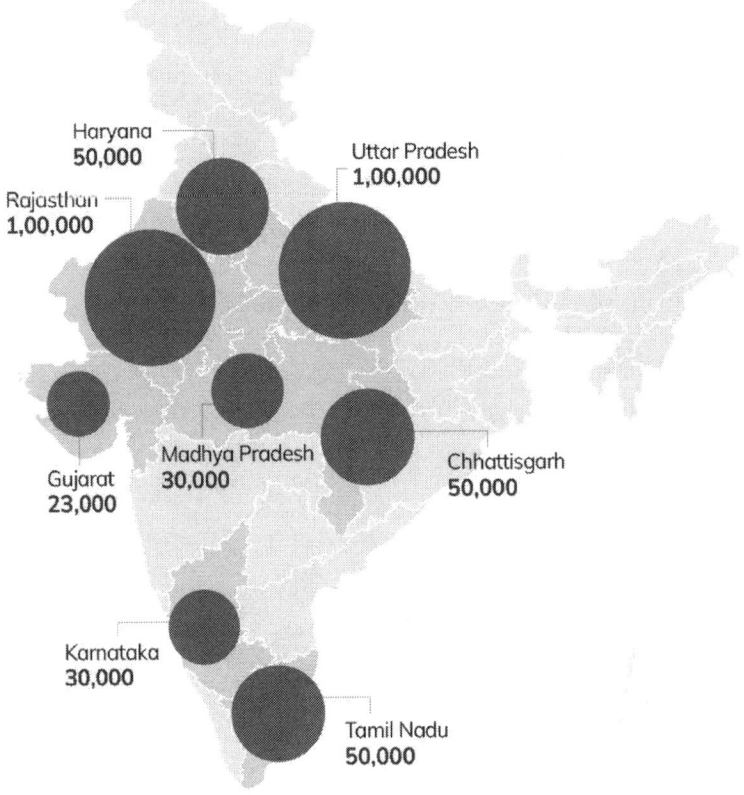

Haryana
50,000

Rajasthan
1,00,000

Uttar Pradesh
1,00,000

Gujarat
23,000

Madhya Pradesh
30,000

Chhattisgarh
50,000

Karnataka
30,000

Tamil Nadu
50,000

Source: State governments and media reports

In addition, since 2018, the Ministry of Culture has been giving grants to temples in the name of 'financial assistance for allied cultural activities'. In response to a parliamentary question, the ministry listed twenty-three sites that had received about ₹18 crore since the inception of the scheme— all Hindu.

CONCLUSION: The hajj subsidy stands cancelled. The Indian state today spends far larger amounts on Hindu religious events, pilgrimages, and temples. Majority appeasement, anyone?

◆

CLAIM: Appeasement is real...because governments are spending lavishly on madrasas

Government spending on minority welfare is a pittance. So was the spending on the hajj subsidy when it existed. From the seemingly bottomless well of Hindutva grievance, however, comes another accusation of appeasement—the state funding of madrasas. The Hindu Right asks: why does the government lavish funds on Muslim religious seminaries to teach the Quran when the Gita cannot be taught in schools? In May 2022, a Hindutva blowhard framed this long-running gripe in starkly ominous terms. In a video that circulated on social media, Pramod Muthalik of the vigilante group Sri Ram Sene delivered a minute-long rant on how funds from Hindu taxpayers were being wasted on Arabic education at madrasas. Ban madrasas, he warned the government, or else his vigilante army might have to take matters into their hands.

It is true that madrasas get government funds in India. The Constitution allows them to.

Article 28 of the Constitution bans religious teaching in institutions wholly funded by the state—that is, in government schools. Madrasas are not government schools—they are private bodies, some of which are part-aided by the government, or have government recognition. Under Article 28, these categories of institutions can offer religious instruction. Part-funded institutions require parental consent to do so.

This is not Muslim appeasement. The article is religion-agnostic—any educational institution can get government aid, no matter who runs it, and can impart religious education with parental approval.

How much government funds do madrasas receive? Nowhere close to Hindutva exaggerations.

Under the Scheme for Providing Quality Education in Madrasas (SPQEM), the main central government scheme for madrasas, ₹1,138 crore has been spent on 21,000 madrasas between 2009 and 2018. This comes to an average of ₹126 crore per year. India's overall school budget in 2018 was ₹50,000 crore.

Even this expenditure is shrinking: the number of teachers supported under the scheme came down from 50,957 in 2015–16 to 12,518 in 2017–18, a drop of 75 per cent.

What is also worth noting here is that SPQEM supports the teaching of maths, science, and social studies in madrasas—not Quranic studies. It does so by providing honorariums for the hiring of teachers of modern subjects.

Some state governments also spend on madrasa education, usually as part of their minority welfare budgets, but the amounts are a small fraction of their school education budgets. We analysed the budgets of ten states with the highest Muslim population shares.

Among them, Bihar's minorities welfare department allocated ₹547 crore for madrasa education in 2023–24, about 4 per cent of the ₹12,906 crore budgeted for primary and secondary education. This was the highest allocation among the ten states. The others ranged between 2.80 per cent for West Bengal, 0.70 per cent for Jharkhand, to 0.05 per cent for Uttarakhand.

The Hindu Right not only overstates the extent of government support to madrasas, but also the scale of them.

According to data shared by the Ministry of Minority

Affairs in 2022, 43.52 lakh students were enrolled in 26,928 madrasas registered with the government. Not all students in madrasas are Muslim. Regardless, this is a small number for a country with the second largest Muslim population in the world: it comes to just 1.64 per cent of the 26.52 crore student enrolment in Indian schools.

There are, of course, madrasas that lie outside the realm of government scrutiny. It is hard to put a number to the students enrolled in such madrasas. However, the Sachar Committee in 2006 cited two estimates—one from the National Council of Applied Economic Research and the other from the National Council of Educational Research and Training—that showed only about 2.3 per cent to 4 per cent of Muslim children attend madrasas.

Exaggerating the madrasa bogey has become a ruse for greater state control of them. In BJP-ruled Uttar Pradesh, for instance, the government has been surveying madrasas, delaying teacher salaries under SPQEM, while simultaneously boasting of funding madrasa modernization. In Assam, also BJP-ruled, government-aided madrasas have been closed down and converted into regular schools.

It would be one thing if the BJP opposed religious education at large. After all, there is a case to be made that state-supported education should be modern and secular.

However, parallel to the demonization of madrasas, there is now a growing promotion of Hindu religious education. Across India, both BJP and Opposition states have promised government support for Hindu religious education in Vedic schools and gurukuls.

At the national level, the centre has cleared the setting up of two Vedic education boards. Students passing out of these boards will be treated on a par with students from other government school boards.

Even Hindu religious texts are entering school and college curricula. In 2022, the education ministers of Gujarat and Himachal Pradesh said the Bhagavad Gita would be made a mandatory part of school curricula. The Gujarat decision was challenged in court, on grounds that it contravened Article 28, which prohibits religious instruction in government schools.

The legal challenge did not stop more BJP-ruled states at the time like Karnataka and Madhya Pradesh from making similar announcements. 'The Ramayana, Mahabharata, Vedas, Upanishads and Bhagavad Gita are invaluable books,' Madhya Pradesh chief minister Shivraj Singh Chouhan said at an RSS event in January 2023. 'These texts have the capacity to make humans moral and complete. We will teach these books in government schools.'

CONCLUSION: The madrasa bogey is exaggerated. Government expenditure on madrasas is a small fraction of overall spending on education.

◆

CLAIM: Appeasement is real because…the Constitution has a pro-Muslim bias

There is no evidence to show that governments have spent inordinate amounts of taxpayer money on Muslims. Where does that leave Muslim appeasement?

The Hindu Right has an answer: appeasement is baked into the Indian Constitution itself.

What is seen as an unfair advantage are cultural and educational protections enshrined in Article 29 and Article 30 of the Indian Constitution. Clause 1 of Article 29 states: 'Any section of citizens residing in the territory of India or any part thereof having a distinct language, script or culture of its own shall have the right to conserve the same.' Clause 1 of Article 30 spells it out more unambiguously: 'All minorities, whether based on religion or language, shall have the right to establish and administer educational institutions of their choice.'

These clauses did not emerge out of a vacuum. Decades before India became independent, its leaders recognized the need to safeguard minorities.

In 1930, Jawaharlal Nehru wrote in *Young India*:

> There is no surer method of rousing the resentment of the minority and keeping it apart from the rest of the nation than to make it feel that it has not got the freedom to stick to its own ways...Therefore we in India must make it clear to all that our policy is based on granting this freedom to the minorities and that under no circumstance will any coercion or repression of them be tolerated. Indeed we should go further and state that it will be the business of the state to give favoured treatment to minority and backward communities.

As Partition loomed, these concerns became more pronounced. But, contrary to the standard Hindutva narrative, Nehru was not the sole 'villain' in enshrining minority safeguards in the Constitution. The final shape of Articles 29 and 30 flowed from the recommendations of the Advisory Committee of the Constituent Assembly on Fundamental Rights. Its chairman was Sardar Vallabhbhai Patel.

In hindsight, it could be argued that India's recognition of minority rights was ahead of its time. The rest of the world took almost four decades to catch up. The United Nations adopted a landmark declaration of minority rights in its General Assembly in 1992. 'States [shall] protect the existence and the national or ethnic, cultural, religious and linguistic identity of minorities within their respective territories and shall encourage conditions for the promotion of that identity. States shall adopt appropriate legislative and other measures to achieve those ends,' the declaration said.

A host of similar charters were adopted around the same time by influential European organizations, underscoring a commitment to minority rights and the need for minority-specific measures. These included declarations by the Organisation for Security and Cooperation in Europe in 1990–91, and the Council of Europe in 1992. The European Union, in 1993, even made respect for minority rights one of the 'accession criteria' for countries that wished to join the union.

In India, meanwhile, Hindutva groups drummed up the idea that minority safeguards amounted to constitutionally sanctioned appeasement, giving minority communities an unfair advantage when it comes to running educational institutions.

Here is why that argument does not hold.

The Constitution does not define minorities. It isn't clear who does. There has been an unresolved debate over whether minority status is determined by the centre or states. Amid this ambiguity, even Hindus have claimed minority status in states where their numbers are small and Hindu-run educational institutions have invoked Article 30 to protect their freedoms.

Take the example of the Dayanand Anglo-Vedic colleges in Punjab, a state where Sikhs outnumber Hindus. These colleges are run by the Arya Samaj, a Hindu reformist movement. In 1971, the DAV went to the Supreme Court against a move by the Punjab government to affiliate all colleges to the Guru Nanak University. According to the DAV petition, the main purpose of the university was to propagate Sikhism and Gurmukhi, the standard script of the Sikhs. The petition argued that as the colleges were run by a religious and linguistic minority in Punjab, this was violative of their rights under

Article 30. The court upheld their claim to minority status, but rejected their contention that their rights were being violated.

Further, the concessions under Article 30 do not apply to institutions run by religious minorities alone, but also Hindu linguistic minorities.

For instance, in 2003, the Supreme Court pronounced a landmark verdict in a case related to the T. M. A. Pai Foundation, a Konkani linguistic minority trust that runs elite educational institutions in Manipal, Karnataka. The foundation invoked its minority status to challenge a new state law that sought to cap the fee it could charge students.

The case resulted in legal boundaries being set for all minority institutions. An eleven-judge bench of the Supreme Court upheld the right of a minority-run educational institution to admit students of its choice, but said it must be subject to a test of reasonableness.

Like the T. M. A. Pai Foundation case, many legal disputes related to Article 30 involve institutions run by Hindu linguistic minority groups. But these aren't the ones that get the Hindu Right worked up—its opposition is limited to institutions run by religious minorities, in particular, Muslims.

CONCLUSION: The special status to minorities under the Constitution is not a Muslim privilege. It applies to countless Hindu linguistic minority institutions as well.

◆

CLAIM: Appeasement is real because...the Congress, pandering to Muslims, is opposed to a Uniform Civil Code

The time was the 1980s. The term 'Muslim appeasement' was, to borrow from the present, going viral.

The trigger for the uproar: the Shah Bano verdict. Shah

Bano was a Muslim woman seeking maintenance from her divorced husband. Her husband contested the claim arguing that under Muslim personal law, maintenance is only paid for a temporary period after divorce.

But the Supreme Court ruled in Shah Bano's favour, holding that civil rights trumped personal law. To placate the Muslim clergy, the Congress government under Prime Minister Rajiv Gandhi passed a legislation that bypassed the Supreme Court verdict. It was a misstep, drawing widespread criticism, including from Muslims. A delegation of Muslim women met the prime minister to register their protest.

The moment was seized by the Hindu Right. The BJP president L. K. Advani popularized the term 'pseudo-secularism', arguing the Congress' secularism was false because the government did not treat all religious communities equally, instead it favoured Muslims. He argued the Shah Bano case was validation for what Hindu groups had long held—that the Congress, from the time of Nehru, had interfered with Hindu personal laws while leaving Muslim personal laws untouched. It is true that Nehru—despite a backlash from Hindu conservatives, including those within his party—had pushed through reforms in Hindu personal laws in the 1950s. But the momentum to reform Hindu laws was building well before Independence, from the period of World War I, not out of anti-Hindu bias.

As historian Eleanor Newbigin writes in *The Hindu Family and the Emergence of Modern India*, the British needed to raise tax revenues which 'required a clear understanding of who owned what'. Muslim laws posed less of a problem since 'the recognition of individual property rights, for women as well as for men, under Muslim law meant that…it seemed to be much closer to the English legal system'. But Hindu laws vested property in a family unit. The British initially found the system hard to comprehend. Then, in 1917, under wartime pressure, they used it to subject Hindu families to higher taxation. This provoked a response from Hindu lawmakers, setting into motion a process to clarify Hindu family structures through legislation. The economic agenda of the British intersected with a reformist impulse within the Hindu community. Indian nationalists were keen to establish that they were capable of fixing their own house, with the first proposal for a code of Hindu family law coming from two legislators in 1921. The proposal didn't go far, but piecemeal measures related to marriage, property, and inheritance built up to the passage of the Hindu Women's Rights to Property Act of 1937, known as the Deshmukh Act, granting inheritance rights to Hindu widows.

Contrary to the arguments of the Hindu Right, Muslim personal laws also underwent reform in the pre-Independence era, with their codification under the Shariat Act of 1937, followed by the Dissolution of Muslim Marriages Act of 1939. As lawyer and historian Rohit De points out, these legislative reforms ensured 'Muslim women could inherit and hold property, maintain a separate legal identity from their husband, were required to give consent to marriages, and could independently sue for divorce in the courts.'

In fact, at that time, some Hindu legislators, including the sole woman legislator, Radhabai Subbarayan, praised Muslim law as more progressive. G. V. Deshmukh, who had shepherded the Deshmukh Act of 1937, went to the extent of saying that if 'Mohammedan society progresses, in future every society in India will follow their example'. In 1941, when the British set up a committee under jurist B. N. Rau to examine matters related to the Deshmukh Act, it instead went on to propose a wider Hindu Code. Reform-minded Hindus backed the effort but conservatives resisted it. The process stalled for a decade, until Nehru's fresh attempt to introduce a Hindu Code Bill in the early 1950s.

Even this attempt was met with fierce opposition—the bill was scrapped, diluted, and ultimately broken into four different legislations before they could be passed.

Till date, the Hindu Right argues that the opposition to Hindu law reform was solely because it was one-sided. Nehru, they argue, should have brought a Uniform Civil Code, a common law governing marriage and succession, meant to replace all personal religious laws. The reason the Congress shied away from doing so, they claim, was because Muslims vigorously opposed a Uniform Civil Code.

This is not entirely incorrect.

Muslim concerns over the Uniform Civil Code came to the fore during a Constituent Assembly debate in November 1948. A Muslim member said it would be 'tyrannous to interfere with the religious practices, and with the religious laws'. The Uniform Civil Code, first proposed by Ambedkar as a fundamental right, was eventually included in the Constitution as a directive principle of state policy, a non-binding guideline for future governments.

But soon the debate resurfaced. When the Hindu Code Bill was introduced in the 1950s, the Hindu Mahasabha sprang up to demand a Uniform Civil Code instead.

In 1954, speaking in Parliament, Nehru said he favoured a Uniform Civil Code. 'But I will confess this: I do not think that at the present moment, the time is ripe in India for my trying to push it through,' he said, a likely acknowledgement of Muslim anxieties in post-Partition India.

The Hindu Right's advocacy of the Uniform Civil Code, however, was called out as insincere by Ambedkar, who wondered how those opposing state interference in religious laws had overnight turned into supporters of a civil code.

The legacy of insincerity carries over till this day. Decades later, despite being in power, the BJP has talked up the need for a Uniform Civil Code but stopped short of introducing one. Many argue the BJP's ambivalence stems from a realization that bringing a code would jeopardize advantages that accrue from Hindu personal laws. For instance, Hindu law sanctions the much-coveted concept of the Hindu Undivided Family (HUF), a family-based taxation unit eligible for tax breaks, a concession not granted to any other religious group. A civil code will bring an end to this provision. In 2018, the National Law Commission, tasked with examining the viability of a Uniform Civil Code, recommended abolishing HUF 'given that it is not congruent with corporate governance, nor is it conducive for the tax regime'. The commission noted that there was a need to weed out discriminatory practices in the personal laws of *all* religious groups. But a Uniform Civil Code was neither 'necessary, desirable or feasible at this stage' to achieve that goal, it said, citing the near-impossibility of fitting India's fragmented, myriad web of personal laws under one umbrella.

Ignoring the law commission's findings, the BJP made the Uniform Civil Code a major poll promise in Uttarakhand elections in 2022. After it came to power, it set up a committee to create a draft civil code. The committee completed its work in July 2023, but its report is yet to be made public.

With national elections looming, the prime minister himself revived discussions on a Uniform Civil Code. Simultaneously, a new Law Commission solicited public views on the matter. Within weeks of the announcement, the commission was flooded with representations from several communities asking to be left out of the ambit of a civil code. These included tribal communities that the BJP considers politically valuable. Media reports suggested that the BJP had decided to go slow on UCC since it fears a political backlash in poll-bound states with significant tribal populations.

This may explain why the BJP has narrowed its rhetoric around a civil code to a single provision of Muslim law—polygamy.

In July 2023, the BJP government in Assam announced its plans to introduce a bill to outlaw polygamy among all communities. In April 2022, the Assam chief minister Himanta Biswa Sarma had said: 'No Muslim woman wants her husband to bring home three other wives'.

Polygamy, or rather polygyny, the practice of having more than one wife, was proscribed among Hindus in the 1950s. A popular perception is that since Muslim personal law allows polygyny, Muslim men have more sexual partners and more children compared to men of other communities, and this has led to Muslim population growing faster than others. (Illogical as it may be, this has helped fuel the 'population jihad' theory, which we have debunked at length in Chapter 2.)

Data shows polygyny isn't just limited to Muslims. The National Family Health Survey found prevalence of polygyny among Muslims was 1.9 per cent, not much higher than the 1.3 per cent among Hindus and 1.6 per cent among other religious groups. Another survey found Hindu men have more partners on average than Muslim men.

CONCLUSION: Muslim anxieties in post-Partition India led the Congress to go slow on a Uniform Civil Code. Subsequently, even the BJP, while drumming up the need for a Uniform Civil Code, has so far fallen short of introducing one—most likely to avoid losing special advantages accruing from Hindu personal law.

EPILOGUE

POWER, FALSEHOODS, AND CONSEQUENCES

For much of their life, the conspiracy theories we have tackled in this book were largely confined to the extreme fringes of the Hindutva ecosystem, only sporadically leaking into the political mainstream.

This is no longer the case.

Today, dangerous, divisive theories aren't just peddled by anonymous trolls on the internet. They are platformed at the highest tiers of political and governmental power, at a scale never seen before.

From ministers to members of Parliament to chief ministers, political VIPs have fanned the worst forms of bigotry, the most outrageous of falsehoods—what we call VIP hate speech. More on this later.

Each of the theories we have debunked in this book— 'love jihad', 'population jihad', forced conversions, Muslim appeasement—has been endorsed and amplified by high-ranking political leaders.

The oxygen of power has made these conspiracy theories more potent, more impactful. The consequences have been deadly.

Nowhere is this better illustrated than a conspiracy theory that unleashed a numbing wave of violence in the country after it was endorsed at the topmost levels of power. We briefly examine it since it vividly demonstrates the dangers of powerful political figures lending their support to divisive fictions.

◆

It was April 2014. India was in the throes of a national election. An inflammatory claim restricted so far to the violent margins of the Hindutva universe entered the political arena. The man platforming it was no marginal figure—he was Narendra Modi, the BJP's prime ministerial candidate.

In speech after speech, he repeatedly referred to the 'pink revolution' engineered by the Congress-led central government.

An election address in Nawada, Bihar, is characteristic of how the PM aspirant built his case. 'The country has heard of a green revolution, of a white revolution,' he said, referring to the advances in agriculture and dairy farming. 'But the government currently in power in Delhi wants neither. It has taken up the cause of a pink revolution.'

'Do you know what it is?' he asked. 'When pashu are killed, they call the colour of the meat pink revolution.'

'In village after village, pashu are being killed, pashu are being stolen.'

'Pashu are being taken to Bangladesh.'

In North India, the term pashu is used interchangeably for livestock and cattle.

A few sentences later, Modi left no doubt about which animal he was referring to: 'The government in Delhi is such that if a farmer or cattle rearer wants a subsidy, it is not ready to give one. But those who butcher gai, butcher pashu, destroy the country's dairy industry, if they set up a slaughterhouse, the government in Delhi gives them a subsidy.'

Gai, or cows, are considered sacred by many Hindus. The spectre of cow slaughter is one of the oldest, deadliest triggers of sectarian fury in India. The last time a lawmaker stoked the subject, his words helped fuel an assault on India's Parliament. The year was 1966. A massive crowd of protestors—some of them sadhus, armed with tridents and spears—marched towards Parliament, demanding a national ban on cow slaughter. Among those egging on the crowds was Swami Rameshwaranand, an MP from the Jan Sangh party, the precursor of the BJP. In an inflammatory speech, he asked the protestors to teach those within the walls of Parliament 'a lesson'.

So perilous was the moment that a senior leader of the same party—Atal Bihari Vajpayee, a future prime minister of India—felt compelled to urge his colleague, the Swami, to withdraw his appeal. It was to no avail. As the surging mob attempted to breach the security cordon around Parliament, chaos ensued. At least six protestors were killed in the police firing. Some accounts say a policeman, too, was killed.

The events of 1966 did not result in a national cow slaughter law. But it sped up the passage of state-level cow protection legislation that banned cow slaughter in all but eight Indian states and union territories. Yet, cattle trade continued, with farmers—predominantly Hindu—selling their aged or infirm cattle at rural markets to traders—mostly Muslims— and using their earnings to purchase productive cattle. 'The "Hindu" farmer never had any issue with the "Muslim" butcher,' journalist Harish Damodaran explained. 'The latter was actually doing a service by taking his unproductive animal and even paying him ₹5,000–10,000 that could, in turn, be used to part-finance a new milch cow for ₹25,000–30,000.' In Hindutva circles, however, this continued to be cast as an Islamic conspiracy to steal and massacre India's cows, a baseless and virulent claim rarely given mainstream political oxygen.

That changed with the 'pink revolution' speeches, an inflammatory mix of half-truths and distortions that connected the fraught subject of cow slaughter to India's burgeoning meat export industry.

It is true that with the emergence of a professionally-run export-dedicated industry, India's meat exports have steadily risen in the past several decades. But India prohibits the export of cow meat. Rather, it exports the meat of the buffalo, which is not classified as beef by the Indian government, even if it is treated as such in some countries. Moreover, the UPA subsidy Modi referred to was for the agri-food export industry as a whole, of which meat export is a component. Yet the 'pink revolution' speeches ended up giving high-profile legitimacy to the violent fantasies of the Hindutva fringe, and signalled to the political class a new licence to amplify divisive falsehoods.

Within months of the BJP's victory in 2014, the drumbeat of the 'cow in peril' rapidly gained ground. In early 2015, BJP-led Maharashtra toughened its cow protection laws. Other BJP states followed suit. Parallel to this, buffalo meat exports continued to rise. So did attacks by gau rakshaks, or self-styled cattle vigilantes, mainly targeting Muslims.

An inflection point came in September 2015 when a Muslim man named Mohammed Akhlaq was beaten to death by his Hindu neighbours on the unfounded suspicion that his family had killed a cow. The attack took place in Uttar Pradesh's Dadri district, at Delhi's doorstep.

The regime's response to the Dadri killing was in keeping with the new normal. BJP leaders spoke up, not to condemn the perpetrators, but to produce rationalizations for the violence. One leader described the killing as the work of 'innocent children' acting out of 'excitement'. Another BJP parliamentarian threatened more vigilantism. 'If someone insults our mother (the cow), we would rather die than tolerate it,' he said. The killing and the ruling party's response sparked a public outcry. The BJP hit back. Too much was being made of an isolated instance of violence, its leaders said. The data tells a different story.

Using media archives on the internet, we counted the number of cow-related attacks across two time periods—from 2009 to 2014, the tenure of the Congress-led UPA government, and from 2014, when the first BJP-led NDA government took oath, to May 2023. More details on our methodology can be found in the endnotes of the book. We found only one instance of cow-related violence between 2009 and 2014. In June 2012, in Punjab's Mansa district, the houses of two factory owners, Ajaib Singh and Mewa Singh, were set ablaze after carcasses of about twenty-five cows were found near the unit. The attack was reportedly led by the VHP. No one was killed.

In contrast, from 2014 to May 2023, we counted 136 such cow-related attacks. At least 66 people were killed and 284 injured. Of those killed, at least 70 per cent were Muslims.

To be clear, relying on media reports to build a data set is an imperfect exercise. It could be argued that the media was not paying attention to cow-related violence before 2014 and digital record-keeping was less comprehensive since the internet was still evolving. But we found that long before 2014, killings in the name of the cow were still considered shocking enough for the media to take note of them. For instance, a mob attack that led to the killings of seven Dalit men in Haryana in 2002 on suspicion that they were skinning a cow was widely reported in newspapers.

The overall trend from our research based on media reports is clear: cow-related violence has witnessed a dramatic spike since 2014.

◆

It is not just violence that followed in the aftermath of the 'pink revolution' speeches. It became increasingly commonplace for ruling party politicians to spotlight other bigoted conspiracy theories lurking in the shadows. Virtually every theory we have debunked in the book has been amplified by people in power, in an unprecedented manner.

We know this from another data set we created using media reports and statements made by politicians on social media. It catalogues instances of hate speech by high-ranking politicians. By hate speech, we mean statements that are communal, casteist, or constitute calls to violence. We also included 'dog whistles'— coded comments against a community. We limited the entries to remarks made by central and state level ministers, members of parliament, members of legislative assemblies, chief ministers, governors, party bosses, and prominent figures in Sangh Parivar organizations.

Like we did with the data set on cow-related violence, we selected two time periods for our analysis: 2009–2014, when the Congress was in government, and 2014–May 2023, when the BJP has been in power. In the Congress years, we counted close to 25 instances of hate speech. That number shot up to over 460 instances of VIP hate speech in the BJP years. Averaging it out, that is a nine-fold jump.

Rising hate speech is bad enough. But, worse, much of it is based on outright lies. For example, ahead of a bye-election in Karnataka in 2020, BJP leader and former deputy chief minister K. S. Eshwarappa declared his party 'won't give tickets to Muslims'—an example of hate speech. In a previous election, he had said 'Young Muslim men are getting involved with Hindu women as part of "love jihad"'. In addition to being hateful, this is false—as we have shown in Chapter 1.

The hateful lies aren't just confined to the ones we have

debunked in this book. New ones keep sprouting. During the years of the COVID-19 pandemic, BJP politicians fuelled baseless talk of a 'corona jihad'.

For instance, Shobha Karandlaje, BJP MP, referring to a gathering at an Islamic centre in Delhi which had seen a high number of COVID cases, said: 'Efforts began at Tablighi Jamaat event in Delhi to spread coronavirus throughout the country. There seems to be "corona jihadi plan" behind that meeting.' Sahender Singh Chauhan, a BJP MLA, went further with the vitriol. 'I appeal to the bank in my constituency to assign a different time for Muslims so that they don't mingle with common people. I urge the public to stay away from people of a certain community in the interest of your family and the nation,' he said. With the pandemic over, the bogey of 'corona jihad' may have died out. But now there is 'land jihad', the spurious theory of a Muslim conspiracy to seize land through fraudulent means, given oxygen by no less than India's home minister Amit Shah. In a public meeting in Assam in March 2021, he promised to bring a law against 'land jihad'.

Constitutional functionaries are not just borrowing Hindutva conspiracy theories—they are now inventing them. In May 2023, Assam chief minister Himanta Biswa Sarma claimed his government was working against 'fertiliser jihad', casting the largely Bengali-Muslim vegetable growers of the state in a sinister light. It is hard to predict how many more such fictions will be spawned by those in power. What's easier to predict is the impact of the hateful lies: an India that no longer belongs equally to all its citizens.

ACKNOWLEDGEMENTS

The authors would like to collectively acknowledge the invaluable contribution of Supriya Kumar to this book. She came on board as a researcher while wrapping up a master's degree in sociology at the Jawaharlal Nehru University. Over time, her role vastly expanded, from delving into historical sources, scouring government databases, to a reporting assignment in Uttar Pradesh. We would like to thank Avinash Singh and the excellent team at How India Lives for helping us visualize data in the book. We are grateful to Pujitha Krishnan for her meticulous editing, Bena Sareen for her thoughtful design, and David Davidar and the team at Aleph for handling the book with such care.

SREENIVASAN JAIN

The idea of this book began out of conversations between Mariyam Alavi and me, then colleagues at NDTV, around three years ago. As television journalists reporting on the surge of Hindutva conspiracies, we felt a book would serve as a more enduring record of our work, compared to the ephemeral nature of TV reportage. We began work on the project in earnest in early 2022. A few months later, Supriya Sharma joined our efforts, greatly expanding the scope and rigour of the book. The journalism that forms the spine of the book builds on the work of the fabulous team of reporters and producers I have had the privilege of working with over the past decade: Niha Masih, Manas Pratap Singh, Manas Roshan,

Sonal Matharu, Shruti Menon, Sukirti Dwivedi, Nimisha Jaiswal, Saurabh Shukla, Aravinth Gunasekar, Ambika Varma, Yamini Joshi, and many more. None of that work would have been possible without Prannoy and Radhika Roy—immense gratitude to them for creating a newsroom where power could be held to account, even in the darkest of times. Further thanks to: Faizan Mustafa, for patiently responding to our multiple requests for clarifications on debates around personal law reform; Vikram Goyal, for his abiding generosity and Ratna Appnender, for casting a sceptical eye on the writing. Finally, to my mother and brother for their enduring love and support.

MARIYAM ALAVI

I would like to thank Sreenivasan Jain, or Vasu as we call him, for roping me into this project with him, and for always being incredibly generous with credit, and Supriya Sharma, who came in like a godsend at a time when we were finding it difficult to juggle work, the book, and life. As Vasu mentioned, thanks are owed to our former colleagues at NDTV, whose work has informed a lot of the reporting that went into this book. To Adila Matra, who was my personal editor and sounding board. My family, especially my mother, who stood by me even through the worst of my mood swings as we delved into some of the darker themes in the book. And my partner, Sehran, who unquestioningly supported all my life and career decisions.

SUPRIYA SHARMA

I used to think that if I ever wrote a book, it would be a long, ponderous text. I must thank Vasu and Mariyam for saving me from that fate. My contribution to the book draws upon the work and insights of the many fantastic colleagues I have had over the years at *Scroll*—Rohan Venkatramakrishnan, Ipsita Chakravarty, Shoaib Daniyal, Aarefa Johari, Sruthisagar Yamunan, Malini Subramaniam, Aishwarya Iyer, and several others. In particular, I would like to thank Arunabh Saikia for reading an early draft related to Assam, and T. A. Ameerudheen for helping me track down and interview a key protagonist in the 2009 'love jihad' case of Kerala. I am grateful to Samir Patil and Naresh Fernandes for building and nurturing the small and fiercely independent newsroom where I work. Special thanks to Naresh for generously granting me the time and space to work on the book, and for guiding the writing as an editor-in-absentia. My parents, family, and friends remain an abiding source of strength.

NOTES

INTRODUCTION

ix   **But go by this Facebook post:** Chanderkant Gautam, Facebook post, 24 September 2013, <https://www.facebook.com/photo?fbid=584920624897554&set=a.35561994116095>.

x   **If this seems fantastical, consider this tweet:** Gourav (@ gourav84721943), Post, X.com, 3 July 2021, <https://twitter.com/Gourav84721943/status/1411289728972771329>.

xiii   **there is even a movie on it, endorsed by the Prime Minister of India:** 'PM Modi backs The Kerala Story, says it shows ugly truth of terrorism', *The News Minute*, 5 May 2023.

CHAPTER 1: 'LOVE JIHAD'

2   **It was in this fraught mix that we had come to report the story:** 'Video | Watch: Truth Vs Hype of Love Jihad', *NDTV.com*, 23 August 2014.

2   **for which we had found no credible evidence in our reporting:** Sreenivasan Jain, 'The Mystery of Kawwal: Were Muzaffarnagar Riots Based on Distortion of Facts?', *NDTV.com*, 14 September 2013.

2   **That is how we met her in her house, her identity concealed:** Section 228A of the Indian Penal Code prohibits revealing of the identity of the victim, to 'prevent social victimisation or ostracism of the victim of a sexual offence.'

4   **a photograph appeared of a coy bride and a somewhat stiff looking groom:** Mohammad Ali, 'For Meerut's "Love Jihad" Couple, 3-year Courtship Ends in "Nikah"', *The Hindu*, 5 December 2015.

5   **accepted he had paid money to the family:** Ishita Bhatia, 'BJP Man Gave Rs 25,000 to Kin of Girl Who Alleged "Love Jihad"', *Times of India*, 15 October 2014.

5   **Only 2.6 per cent of marriages in India are interreligious:** Vijdan Mohammad Kawoosa, 'Age, Caste, Job, Education: What

Data on Couples in India Shows', *Hindustan Times*, 3 October 2018.

6   **a riot erupting in the town of Mathura in Uttar Pradesh:** Charu Gupta, 'Hindu Women, Muslim Men: Love Jihad and Conversions', *Economic and Political Weekly*, Vol. 44, No. 51, December 2009.

7   **The violence is endorsed by high-ranking politicians:** 'Ramgarh MLA Gyandev Ahuja Courts Controversy Over Love Jihad', *Times of India*, 2 August 2018.

7   **fifty public marches were taken out against 'love jihad':** Nayonika Bose, Zeeshan Shaikh, Alok Deshpande, '4 Months, 50 Rallies in Maharashtra, One Theme: "*Love Jihad*", "*Land Jihad*" and Economic Boycott', *Indian Express*, 19 March 2023; Tabassum Barnagarwala, 'How "Love Jihad" Rallies Are Spreading Hate Against Muslims in Maharashtra', *Scroll.in*, 10 March 2023.

7   **in response to a parliamentary query in 2020:** 'Starred Question No. 23', *Lok Sabha Answers*, 4 February 2020, <https://pqals.nic.in/annex/173/AS23.pdf>.

7   **known as anti-'love jihad' laws:** Haryana Becomes 11th State to Table "Love Jihad" Law, Congress Protests in Assembly', *The Wire*, 5 March 2022; Banerjee Tirtho, 'Why Maharashtra wants to join states that have laws against "Love Jihad"', *India Today*, 28 December 2022

8   **the Hindu Janajagruti Samiti, a Hindutva organization, first began to use the term:** Shahina K. K., 'The Roots and Evolution of the Myth of "Love Jihad" in Kerala', *Outlook*, 12 April 2023.

8   **at the Catholic Bishops Council in Kerala in 2009:** Rohan Venkataramakrishnan, 'How Real Is the Threat of Love Jihad?', *Scroll.in*, 14 August 2014.

8   **the term made its first official appearance:** *Shahan Sha and Ors. vs State of Kerala*, Bail Application No. 5288, 9 December 2009.

8   **two men petitioned the court:** *Jacob Thomas and Ors. vs Director General of Police and Ors*, Criminal Writ Petition No. 317, 7 August 2009.

8   **The men feared their daughters had been entrapped:** *Jacob Thomas and Ors. vs Director General of Police and Ors.*

8   **Both Mithula Madhavan and Bino Jacob were 23-year-old students:** *Shahan Sha and Ors vs Assistant Commissioner of Police and Ors*, Criminal Miscellaneous Application No. 3836 and 3837, 25

November 25 2009.

8   **the Kerala High Court directed the police:** *Jacob Thomas and Ors. vs Director General of Police and Ors*, Order dated August 12.

8   **Nine days later, the women appeared in court**: Ibid, August 21.

8   **The women told the judges that they were in love**: Ibid, August 26.

8   **'it is only with much persuasion exercised by us…'**: Ibid.

8   **Among the conditions laid down by the judge**s: Ibid, August 21.

9   **the young men rushed back to the court**: Ibid, August 26.

9   **they took a completely different stand**: Ibid.

9   **'The reasons that prompt the alleged detenues to change their stand…'**: Ibid.

9   **an account that also features in a petition he filed in the court**: *Shahan Sha and Ors. vs Assistant Commissioner of Police and Ors.*

9   **Shahan Sha himself was the district president**: Ibid.

10   **'I was born into a lot of problems…'**: Email dated 5 March 2008, Annexure in *Shahan Sha and Ors. vs Assistant Commissioner of Police and Ors*, Criminal Miscellaneous Application No. 3836 and 3837, 25 November 2009.

10   **'Didn't Shachettan tell me once…'**: Email dated 12 May 2008, Annexure in *Shahan Sha and Ors. vs Assistant Commissioner of Police and Ors*, Criminal Miscellaneous Application No. 3836 and 3837, 25 November 2009.

10   **'You should forgo any plans to abandon me'**: Ibid.

10   **the women's parents took them out of college**: *Jacob Thomas and Ors. vs Director General of Police and Ors.*

10   **But they managed to stay in touch with Shahan Sha**: *Shahan Sha and Ors vs Assistant Commissioner of Police and Ors.*

10   **They wanted to leave home and go to Ponnani**: Ibid.

11   **They met a lawyer who advised them to get married**: Ibid.

11   **the women converted to Islam and married the men**: Deed of Agreement to marry, 12 August 2009, Annexure, *Shahan Sha and Ors. vs Assistant Commissioner of Police and Ors.*, Criminal Miscellaneous Application No. 3836 and 3837, 25 November 2009.

12   **He also rejected Shahan Sha and Sirajudeen's withdrawal petitions**: *Shahan Sha and Ors. vs The State of Kerala.*

13   **'I know you was looking for a freedom from parents…'**:

Email dated 13 August 2009, Annexure in *Shahan Sha and Ors. vs Assistant Commissioner of Police and Ors.*, Criminal Miscellaneous Application No. 3836 and 3837, 25 November 2009.

13	**highlighting that the police investigation itself was biased**: *Shahan Sha and Ors. vs Assistant Commissioner of Police and Ors.*

13	**'Conduct of the Investigating Officer shocks the judicial conscience'**: *Shahan Sha and Ors. vs Assistant Commissioner of Police and Ors.*, Criminal Miscellaneous Application No 3836 and 3837, Nov 25. 2009, Common order dated 17 December 2009.

14	**They did so by submitting 'refer reports'**: Ibid, Common order dated 1 December 2010.

14	**'Petitions are dismissed as infructuous'**: Ibid.

15	**Akhila converted to Islam, became Hadiya:** *Asokan K.M. vs The State of Kerala*, WP Crl. No. 25 of 2016, 25 January 2016, <https://indiankanoon.org/doc/110567582/>.

16	**To prepare for the exam, Hadiya took a course:** T.A. Ameerudheen 'Ground Report: How Akhila Became Hadiya – and Why Her Case Has Reached the Supreme Court', *Scroll.in*, 30 August 2017.

16	**She met and married her husband**: Shaju Philip, 'Her Journey From Akhila to Become Hadiya', *Indian Express*, 26 August 2017.

16	**'The strength of our Constitution lies in…'**: *Shafin Jahan vs Asokan K.M. and Ors.* S.L.P. (Crl.) No. 5777 of 2017, 8 March 2018, <https://main.sci.gov.in/supremecourt/2017/19702/19702_2017_Judgement_08-Mar-2018.pdf>.

16	**NIA's probe had not unearthed any proof of conspiracy**: Rajesh Ahuja, 'NIA Ends Kerala Probe, Says There's Love but No Jihad', *Hindustan Times*, 18 October 2018.

17	**Soon, social media was awash with posts**: Displaced Kashmiri Sikhs Conference, Facebook post, 26 June 2021, <https://www.facebook.com/permalink.php?story_fbid=pfbid02X6MSZp BN2WF5g MZCjcLkASSCsA1hC4prDcEZ ah9M4nofNdXL3oXqYCBs9X teQztDl&id=100418667146226>.

18	**In a series of tweets, Sirsa urged**: Manjinder Singh Sirsa (@ mssirsa), 'We will not tolerate forced Nikah and conversions of Sikh daughters living in Kashmir who are forced to marry elderly of different religion Sikhs living in J&K urge @AmitShah for a law that mandates permission of Parents in inter-religion marriages.', X Post, 27 June 2021, <https://twitter.com/mssirsa/

status/1409102988006 678534?s=20>; Manjinder Singh Sirsa (@ mssirsa), Post, 'The local Sikh community of Jammu and Kashmir urges @AmitShah Ji to get a strong law implemented in Jammu & Kashmir (Just like Uttar Pradesh & Madhya Pradesh) mandating Permission of parents in inter-religion marriages to stop these forced Nikahs of Sikh minority girls.', X.com, 27 June 2021, <https:// twitter.com/mssirsa/status/1409058166080348163?s=20>.

18   **'So what if I am young? No one forced me'**: 'Video | Love Jihad Bogey: Kashmir Edition', *NDTV.com*, 1 July 2021.

18   **Sirsa, the politician, posted a celebratory tweet**: Manjinder Singh Sirsa (@mssirsa), Post, 'Paying obeisance at Gurdwara Sri Bangla Sahib with Manmeet Kaur, the Sikh daughter from Kashmir who was forcibly converted. But her family fought for faith and got her back. Manmeet Kaur has come to Delhi to take Guru Sahib's blessings and thank the Sangat for their support', X.com, 29 June 2021, <https://twitter.com/ mssirsa/status/14098 75630984937473?lang=en>.

19   **'I was warned that I would get killed…'**: Jehangir Ali, 'J&K 'Conversion' Row: Sikh Woman 'Handed Over' to Kin Remarries', *The Quint*, 29 June 2021.

19   **'There is no question of "love jihad" at gunpoint…'**: 'Video | Love Jihad Bogey: Kashmir Edition.'

19   **Social media was aflame**: हिंदू राष्ट्र हिंदुत्व की पहचान, Facebook post, 14 November 2022, <https://www.facebook.com/ Tulsigyan/posts/pfbid034tFqqf8AcqZpTjpcotKrrCQpKdxQL tpKZA5tX3LCYDVfgFvZjmYJ6P8gEHv7stpMl>.

21   **'There are many other stories like that of Aaftab and Shraddha…'**: ANI (@ANI), '#WATCH | Gujarat: Aftaab Killed Shardha and Chopped Her Body Into 35 Pieces. When Police Asked Why He Brought Only Hindu Girls He Said He Did It Because They're emotional. There're Other Aftaab-Shradha Too, Country Needs Strict Law Against 'Love Jihaad': Assam CM HB Sarma in Dhansura', X.com, 22 November 2022, <twitter.com/ ANI/status/1595032620219318272>.

21   **30 per cent of married women aged 18–49 have faced spousal violence**: International Institute for Population Sciences, *National Family Health Survey 2019-21 (NFHS-5)*, Ministry of Health and Family Welfare, Government of India, March 2022, <http://rchiips.org/nfhs/NFHS-5_FCTS/India.pdf>.

22   **Sahil Gehlot was accused of strangling his live-in partner**:

Sakshi Chand, 'Nikki Yadav Murder Case: Cop among 4 Who Helped Sahil Gehlot Stash Body in Fridge', *Times of India*, 19 February 2023.

22   **Hardik Shah was charged with killing his live-in partner**: Mohamed Thaver, 'Mumbai: Man Kills Live-in Partner, Hides Body in Box before Calling Scrap Dealer', *Indian Express*, 15 February 2023.

22   **the Facebook page 'Girls - Beware of Love Jihad'**: Girls - Beware of Love Jihad, Facebook post, 30 December 2022, <https://www.facebook.com/GirlsBewareofLoveJihad/posts/pfbid0fQ1KJzhE3odVn7kwdv7vYR9ZD1rfKGhWL7 7v57KcgZ9UipQueJDxi47x323jDvV8l>.

24   **Kumar had described this strategy as 'demographic invasion'**: Vishwa Hindu Parishad – VHP, Facebook Post, 'Press Release, Love Jihad' special issue of VHP's national magazine 'Hindu Vishwa', 25 September 2020, <https://www.facebook. com/VHPDigital/posts/press- releaselove-jihad-is-a-demographic-invasion-alok-kumarlist-of-147-case- stu/2970710169701676/>.

27   **in February 2022, police arrested Ramesh Chandra Swain**: Romita Datta, 'How Odisha 'Conman' Ramesh Chandra Swain Faked Identity, Married 18 Women', *India Today*, 27 February 2022.

27   **the list featured an *OpIndia* article from June 2019**: OpIndia Staff 'लव जिहाद: 3 बच्चों का बाप इमरान बना कबीर शर्मा, ब्राह्मण लड़की से शादी कर दहेज में लिया ₹11 लाख,' *OpIndia*, 6 June 2019.

27   **The report cited a video released by the woman**: 'Man Detained for Hiding Identity for Second Marriage in Sikar District', *Times of India*, 5 June 2019.

27   **It is a pro-Hindutva website**: Ashwine Kumar Singh, 'OpIndia Is Caught Peddling Fake News. Again', *Newslaundry*, 12 November 2022; Ayush Tiwari, 'OpIndia: Hate Speech, Vanishing Advertisers, and an Undisclosed BJP Connection', *Newslaundry*, 23 June 2020.

28   **the murder was the result of the 'rise of testosterone…'**: Lovely Reddy, '23-year Old Hindu Girl Stabbed as She Refused Sexy Ramadan Marriage Proposal', *hinduexistence.org*, 15 June 2017, <hinduexistence.org/2017/06/15/23-year-old-hindu-girl-stabbed-as-she-refused-sexy-ramadan-marriage-proposal>.

28   **The headline of the report used the term 'love story'**: Mritunjay, 'Love Story: प्यार की परीक्षा देने प्रेमी के साथ भागी छात्रा, परिजनों ने लगाया लव जिहाद का आरोप, सांप्रदायिक तनाव", *Dainik Jagran*, 25 February 2020.

29   **Our report went viral**: Alavi, Mariyam, 'With No Credible
        Evidence, 'Love Jihad' Cases in Kanpur Crumble', *NDTV.com*, 28
        November 2021

30   **the provisions of the Special Marriage Act**: The Special
        Marriage Act, 1954, <https://lddashboard.legislative.gov.in/ sites/
        default/files/A1954-43_1.pdf>.

30   **Entire anti-'love jihad' ecosystems have sprung up**: Abhishek
        Dey, 'Court Informers and Mohalla Spies: How Hindutva Groups
        in North India Stop Inter-faith Marriages', *Scroll.in*, 5 August 2018;
        Sandeep Rai and Anusha Jaiswal, '"Love Jihad" and the "social
        Network" — How Interfaith Couples Are Tracked', *The Times of
        India*, 12 December 2020.

31   **The post asked local Hindu groups**: Arvind Singh Rss,
        Facebook post, 21 April 2022, <https://www.facebook. com/
        groups/655900358589481/posts/1123803545132491/>.

31   **'I warn those who conceal identity…'**: 'Yogi Warning: End
        Love Jihad, or Get Ready for Ram Naam Satya Hai', *Indian
        Express*, 31 October 2020.

31   **a clause making conversion by marriage or for marriage
        unlawful**: THE HIMACHAL PRADESH FREEDOM OF
        RELIGION ACT, 2019, 'Section 3: "No person shall convert or
        attempt to convert, either directly or otherwise, any other person
        from one religion to another by use of misrepresentation, force,
        undue influence, coercion, inducement or by any fraudulent
        means or by marriage; nor shall any person abet or conspire such
        conversion"' HP: <https://himachal.nic.in/WriteReadData/
        1892s/10_1892s/THE%20HIMACHAL%20PRADESH%20
        FREEDOM%20OF%20   RELIGION%20ACT%20%2013%20
        of%202019-95744581.pdf>; The Uttar Pradesh Prohibition
        of Unlawful Conversion of Religion Act, 2021, 'Section 3:
        "No person shall convert or attempt to convert, either directly
        or otherwise, any other person from one religion to another
        by use or practice of misrepresentation, force, undue influence,
        coercion, allurement or by any fraudulent means. No person shall
        abet, convince or conspire such conversion. Explanation: For
        the purposes of this sub-section conversion by solemnization of
        marriage or relationship in the nature of marriage on account
        of factors enumerated in this sub-section shall be deemed
        included"', <https://prsindia.org/files/bills_acts/acts_states/uttar-
        pradesh/2021/Act%20No%203%20of%202021%20UP.pdf>.

33   **'We have come across incidents…'**: The Uttarakhand Freedom
        of Religion Act, 2018. <https://prsindia.org/ files/bills_acts/acts_
        states/uttarakhand/2018/Act%2028%20of%202018%20   UKD.
        pdf>.

33   **'interferes with the intricacies of marriage…'**: Jamiat
        Ulama-e-Hind Gujarat vs The State of Gujarat, SCA No. 10304
        of 2021, 19 August 2021, <https://www.theleaflet.in/wp-content/
        uploads/2021/08/SCA103042021_GJHC240320002021_3_
        19082021.pdf>.

33   **the Allahabad High Court said**: Mayra Alias Vaishnvi Vilas
        Shirshikar and Aur. *vs* The State of Uttar Pradesh and Ors, WC
        No. 14896 of 2021, <https://www.livelaw.in/pdf_upload/
        interfaith-marriage-allahabad-hc-404306.pdf>.

34   **the Madhya Pradesh High Court in an interim order held**:
        Umang Poddar, 'Why The Madhya Pradesh High Court Struck
        Down a Law That Restricted Inter-faith Marriages', *Scroll.in*, 22
        November 2022.

34   **'All conversions cannot be said to be illegal'**: 'All Conversion
        Cannot Be Illegal': SC While Refusing to Stay MP High Court
        Order', *The Wire*, 4 January 2023.

34   **States are using the laws to crack down**: Iram Siddique, '3
        months of MP 'love jihad' law: 21 cases, couple knew each other in
        over half ', *Indian Express*, 20 March 2021.

35   **It said the police had registered 427 cases**: 'U.P. says 427
        conversion-related cases were reported under new Act', *The Hindu*,
        12 May 2023.

37   **she had willingly gone with Jibrail**: Neetu's statement as
        recorded by the judicial magistrate of Sitapur under section 164 of
        the CrPC, Chandbibi *vs* The State of Uttar Pradesh, Bail No. 2426
        of 2021, 24 March 2021.

39   **she had left home of her own volition**: A summary of
        statements made by Asha under Section 161 and 164 of CrPC, as
        recorded in an order by the judicial magistrate of Bareilly on 23
        October 2019.

39   **Parul told the police she knew Nadeem**: 'FIR Under "Love
        Jihad" Ordinance: UP Police Finds No Evidence Against Nadeem;
        Charge Dropped', *The Leaflet*, 8 January 2021.

39   **She alleged that her husband had falsely implicated
        Nadeem**: Omar Rashid, 'U.P. Drops Charges Against Muslim
        Man After Finding "No Evidence of Unlawful Conversion"', *The*

Hindu, 7 January 2021.

40   **'There is no material before us...'**: Nadeem *vs* State of Uttar Pradesh and Ors, Cr. Misc. Writ Petition No. 16302 of 2020, 18 December 2020.

40   **A month later, the court recorded**: Ibid.

40   **Shabab was in a long-running affair with Ayushi**: Sabah Gurmat, 'One Year Later: Misuse of "Love Jihad" – 14 Family Members and Peers Arrested Along With the Accused Secure Bail', *The Leaflet*, 28 January 2022.

42   **In a statement to the magistrate**: Azad *vs* The State of Uttar Pradesh, Bail Application No. 170/2021, 27 January 2021.

42   **'It is a fact that the two were in love...'**: Ananya Bhardwaj, '"We Step in When Our Women Step Out With Muslim Men"— How UP Law Empowers Hindu Bully Groups', *ThePrint*, 26 December 2020.

43   **'Thanks to the law, we can operate freely'**: Ibid.

CHAPTER 2: POPULATION JIHAD

44   **'We are also a decaying race...'**: U.N. Mukerji, *A Dying Race,* Calcutta: Bhaskar Mukerjee, 1909, pp. 4 and 97.

44   **Hindus make up 79.80 per cent of the country's population**: 2011 Census of India, Office of the Registrar General and Census Commissioner of India, Government of India, 2011.

45   **Narendra Modi, then chief minister of Gujarat, had called relief camps**: 'Should We Run Relief Camps? Open Child Producing Centres?', *Outlook*, 3 February 2022.

45   **'It should not be the case that...'**: Yogi Adityanath (@ myogiadityanath), "विश्व जनसंख्या दिवस के अवसर पर लखनऊ में 'जनसंख्या स्थिरता पाखवाड़ा' का शुभारंभ..." X.com, 11 July 2022, <https://twitter.com/myogiadityanath/status/154635687197962 6496?s=20>.

45   **'The doctrine of Islam is based upon...'**: Gopal Goswami, 'Fighting Population Jihad: Rising Muslim Population Is Causing Demographic Imbalance, Spells Trouble for Bharat', *Organiser*, 1 September 2021.

45   **an image of a Muslim man riding a scooter with six family members:** Aqib Pathan, 'Old Image From Bangladesh Shared With Demands of Population Control Law in India - Alt News', *Alt News*, 22 September 2020; A. Soni (ashutoshsoni888), Post, 'Kagaz nhi dikhayege| Par population badayge | Subsidy hum khayege | Our last m Hum Dhekenge

|', X.com, 18 Jan. 2020, <https://twitter.com/ashutoshsoni888/status/1218378505546690560>.

47   **Hindus today are about 79.80 per cent of the population**: 2011 Census of India.

47   **India's Hindu population share at 84.98 per cent**: 1961 Census of India, Office of the Registrar General and Census Commissioner of India, Government of India, 1961.

47   **India's Hindu population share had slipped below 80 per cent**: 2011 Census of India.

48   **Muslims grew by 386.37 per cent**: 1961 Census of India; 2011 Census of India.

48   **Muslim women are having more children than Hindu women**: International Institute for Population Sciences, National Family Health Survey 2019-21 (NFHS-5), Ministry of Health and Family Welfare, Government of India, March 2022, <rchiips.org/nfhs/NFHS-5Reports/ NFHS-5_INDIA_REPORT.pdf>.

49   **Hindu population growth rate came down from 20.35 per cent to 16.76 per cent**: 2001 Census of India, Office of the Registrar General and Census Commissioner of India, Government of India, 2001; 2011 Census of India.

49   **The Muslim share in India's population, according to him, will settle at 18.8 per cent**: P. N. Mari Bhat, A. J. Francis Zavier, 'Role of Religion in Fertility Decline', *Economic and Political Weekly*, Vol. 40, No. 5, January 2005.

51   **The Indian Council of Social Science Research had funded the book**: A. P. Joshi, et al, *Religious Demography of India*, Centre for Policy Studies, 2003.

51   **counted among its trustees key ideologues of the BJP-RSS**: 'Trustees', *Centre for Policy Studies*, <cpsindia.org/index.php/trustees>.

52   **'Hindus reduced to a minority in Akhand Bharat...'**: D. Jayaraj and S. Subramanian, 'Abusing Demography', *Economic and Political Weekly*, Vol. 39, No. 12, 20 March 2004.

52   **The authors dismissed the criticism**: A. P. Joshi, et al, 'Blinkered Approach to Demography', *Economic and Political Weekly*, Vol. 39, No. 19, 8 May 2004.

53   **'Government will not give us [Muslims] jobs anyway...'**: 'Govt Not Providing Jobs to Muslims Anyway; AIUDF Chief on Assam's Two Child Policy', *ABP News*, 28 October 2019.

53   **'Do not kill your children for fear of poverty...'**: 'Surah

Al-An'am - 151-165 - Quran.com', *Quran.com*, <quran.com/al-anam/151-165>.

53   **It is actually a condemnation of infanticide**: Qutub Jahan Kidwai, 'Badruddin Ajmal Is Wrong on Islam and Family Planning: Reason Along With Faith Enables Us to Liberate Ourselves From Ignorance', *New Age Islam*, 5 November 2019, <www.newageislam.com/islamic-ideology/qutub-jahan-kidwai/badruddin-ajmal-wrong-islam-family-planning-reason-along-with-faith-enables-liberate-ourselves- ignorance/d/120193>.

53   **'Nowhere has the Quran prohibited family planning...'**: S.Y. Quraishi, *The Population Myth: Islam, Family Planning and Politics in India*, Gurugram: HarperCollins India, 2015.

54   **There are divergent views among Indian Muslims on contraception**: Ibid.

54   **By 2019–21, it had increased to 60.20 per cent**: International Institute for Population Sciences, National Family Health Survey 1998-99 (NFHS-2), Ministry of Health and Family Welfare, Government of India, October 2000, <http://rchiips.org/nfhs/data/india/ indintro.pdf>; National Family Health Survey 2019-21 (NFHS-5).

54   **more Muslim men (34.10 per cent) use contraception than Hindu men (32.70 per cent)**: National Family Health Survey 2019-21 (NFHS-5).

54   **rate of female sterilization among Muslims has improved to 21.80 per cent**: National Family Health Survey 1998-99 (NFHS-2); National Family Health Survey 2019-21(NFHS-5).

56   **two Muslim-majority regions, have some of the lowest fertility rates**: National Family Health Survey 2019-21 (NFHS-5).

56   **So are women who have never been to school**: Ibid.

57   **Muslims in Tamil Nadu, Andhra Pradesh, and Telangana have a lower fertility rate**: Ibid

58   **Pragya Thakur, a member of Parliament from the Bharatiya Janata Party**: '2008 Malegaon blast: Key witness declared hostile, 37th so far', *Scroll.in,* 11 May 2023

58   **According to Thakur, they were arriving in India in hordes:** Rajendra Sharma, 'Pragya Singh Thakur Demands Population Control Bill, Uniform Civic Code in India', *Times of India*, 11 July 2021.

58   **he compared illegal immigrants to 'termites'**: Devjyot

Ghoshal, 'Amit Shah Vows to Throw Illegal Immigrants Into Bay of Bengal', *Reuters*, 12 April 2019.

58   **government would prepare a National Register of Citizens to weed them out**: 'Centre Plans NRC Exercise All Over the Country: Amit Shah', *The Hindu*, 20 November 2019.

58   **responses to parliamentary questions about illegal immigrants**: Lok Sabha Answers: 'Starred Question No. 168', Lok Sabha Answers, 3 March 2020. 'Unstarred Question No. 3831', Lok Sabha Answers, 16 July 2019. 'Starred Question No. 150', Lok Sabha Answers, 2 July 2019. 'Unstarred Question No. 1680', Lok Sabha Answers, 2 July 2019. 'Unstarred Question No. 1744', Lok Sabha Answers, 2 July 2019. 'Unstarred Question No. 1292', Lok Sabha Answers, 18 December 2018. 'Unstarred Question No. 4121', Lok Sabha Answers, 20 March 2018. 'Unstarred Question No. 687', Lok Sabha Answers, 19 December 2017. 'Starred Question No. 225', Lok Sabha Answers, 1 August 2017. 'Unstarred Question No. 6055', Lok Sabha Answers, 11 April 2017. 'Unstarred Question No. 3217', Lok Sabha Answers, 21 March 2017. 'Starred Question No. 294', Lok Sabha Answers, 6 December 2016. 'Starred Question No. 327', Lok Sabha Answers, 22 December 2015. 'Unstarred Question No. 4569', Lok Sabha Answers, 21 April 2015. 'Starred Question No. 39', Lok Sabha Answers, 25 November 2014. 'Starred Question No. 119', Lok Sabha Answers, 15 July 2014.

60   **'…around 20 million illegal Bangladeshi migrants staying in India.'**: 'Unstarred Question No. 55', *Rajya Sabha Answers*, 16 November 2016.

60   **When it comes to Rohingyas, in 2017, Rijiju said**: 'Unstarred Question No. 1033', *Rajya Sabha Answers*, 27 December 2017.

60   **500 Rohingyas have been given long term visas by the Home Ministry**: Kanishka Singh, 'Here Is How Various Refugee Communities Have Fared in India', *Indian Express*, 14 September 2017.

61   **'justified on grounds of well-founded fear of persecution…'**: Ministry of Home Affairs, 'Law For Refugees in India', Press Information Bureau, Government of India, 6 August 2014, <pib.gov.in/newsite/ PrintRelease.aspx?relid=108152>.

61   **Rohingyas in question would be held in detention centres**: 'Hardeep Singh Puri Hails Govt's Decision to Shift Rohingya Refugees to EWS Flats in New Delhi', *ThePrint*, 17 August 2022.

62   **Between 2001 and 2011, Assam's population grew by 17.07 per cent**: 2011 Census of India.

62   **Go back forty years—the state's population growth rate has been lower**: 'A-2: Decadal Variation in Population since 1901', 2011 Census of India, Office of the Registrar General and Census Commissioner of India, Government of India, 2011. The Census exercise was not conducted in Assam in 1981, as the Assam agitation was at its peak at the time. The population figures and growth rates for 1981 are based on an interpolation exercise carried out by the Census officials.

62   **Between 1901 and 1971, Assam's population grew at a faster pace than India's**: 'A-2: Decadal Variation in Population since 1901', 2011 Census of India.

64   **'Where there is a wasteland thither flock the Mymensinghias…'**: 1931 Census of India, Office of the Registrar General and Census Commissioner of India, Government of India, 1931.

64   **The British encouraged farmers from undivided Bengal to move to Assam**: Arupjyoti Saikia, *The Quest for Modern Assam: A History, 1942-2000*, Gurugram: Penguin Random House India, 2023.

64   **of the 13 lakh migrants who had entered Assam**: 1931 Census of India.

65   **'Prolific breeders and industrious cultivators…'**: 1931 Census of India.

65   **The gap between the population growth rates of Assam and India narrowed down**: Saikia, *The Quest for Modern Assam*, To prepare for the war, the government launched a "grow more food" campaign, which brought more cultivators from Bengal to Assam.

65   **it was impossible to gauge the extent of the immigration**: Assistant Director of Census Operations, Assam, Census of India 1971, Series 3, General Report Part I-A, Assam, Government of India, 31 December 1977.

65   **It treated Hindu migrants from East Pakistan as 'refugees'**: Abdul Mannan, *Infiltration: Genesis of the Assam Movement*, India, SAS Publishers, 2017.

65   **1.78 lakh people 'were either deported or had voluntarily left' Assam between 1961–66**: White Paper on Foreigners' Issue, Home and Political Department, Government of Assam, 12 October

2020.

65   **those expelled in the 1960s were Muslim**: Vani Kant Borooah, 'The Killing Fields of Assam: Myth and Reality of Its Muslim Immigration', *Economic and Political Weekly*, Vol. 48, No. 4, 16 January 2013.

65   **between 1961–71, the Muslim population growth rate in Assam dropped below the Hindu rate**: 1971 Census of India, Office of the Registrar General and Census Commissioner of India, Government of India, 1971.

67   **several states had a higher Muslim population growth than Assam**: Mannan, *Infiltration: Genesis of the Assam Movement*.

69   **The districts reporting higher Muslim population growth rates**: Sagnik Chowdhury, and Abantika Ghosh, 'Assam Muslim Growth Is Higher in Districts Away From Border', *Indian Express*, 30 August 2015.

69   **Muslims in Assam have a higher fertility rate than Hindus**: International Institute for Population Sciences, National Family Health Survey 2019-21 (NFHS-5), Assam, Ministry of Health and Family Welfare, Government of India, Apr. 2021, <rchiips.org/ nfhs/NFHS-5Reports/ Assam.pdf>.

69   **living in the state before 25 March 1971**: 25 March 1971 is when the Bangladesh Liberation War began. As those fleeing the war poured into Assam, it sparked an anti-foreigners movement which ended with the signing of the 1985 Assam Accord. According to the accord, anyone who entered Assam after the midnight of 24 March 1971 was to be considered an illegal immigrant. The NRC borrowed the cut- off date from the accord; Ipsita Chakravarty, 'Explainer: What exactly is the National Register of Citizens?', *Scroll.in*, 15 July 2019.

70   **a smaller fraction of the population in Muslim-majority border districts:** Arunabh Saikia, "Hindus Have Been Disproportionately Targeted': Why the Assam Government Is Not Happy With the NRC', *Scroll.in*, 4 August 2019.

70   **The track record of these tribunals till October 2019**: 'Unstarred Question No. 3558', *Lok Sabha Answers*, 10 December 2019.

70   **Hindutva organizations and the ruling BJP have asked for a recount**: Himanta Biswa Sarma (@himantabiswa), 'I reiterate that as requested by Central and State governments at least 20% reverification (bordering districts) and 10% re-verification

(remaining districts) should be allowed by Honble Apex court for a correct and fair NRC', X.com, 31 August 2019; Ipsita Chakravarty, 'Is the final NRC published in Assam unravelling under political pressure?', *Scroll.in*, 27 October 2020.

CHAPTER 3: FORCED CONVERSIONS

71 **At the heart of the series was a sting operation-style exposé**: 'MLA Goolihatti Shekar Helpless Over His Mother Puttama Converted to Christianity', YouTube, 5 March 2021, <www.youtube.com/watch?v=sKN8n37DQhI>.

71 **A Bangalore-based media watchdog shot off a complaint**: 'Complaint (13-03-2021): Complaint Against Asianet Suvarna News for the "Mahaexclusive and Cover Story"', *Campaign Against Hate Speech*, 14 March 2021, <hatespeechbeda.wordpress. com/2021/03/14/complaint-13-03-2021-complaint-against-asianet-suvarna-news-for-the-mahaexclusive- and-cover-story>.

72 **The MLA himself brought up his mother's conversion**: 'Karnataka Legislative Assembly House Proceedings | 15th Assembly | 10th Session | Live | 21-09-2021', YouTube, 21 September 2021, <www. youtube.com/watch?v=wsl9vx-FaDw>.

72 **announced the Astate government's plan to introduce a law**: Ralph Alex Arakal, 'Ready to meet CM Bommai again on anti-conversion law: Bangalore Archbishop', *Indian Express*, 25 October 2021; 'Karnataka Government Planning to Introduce Law to Ban Forceful Religious Conversions: Bommai', *Indian Express*, 28 September 2021.

72 **The state government claimed the law was not targeted at Christians**: Johnson T. A., 'Karnataka Anti-conversion Law: House Debates if Hate, Like Love, "Inborn", or Is It "Motivated, Man-made"', *Indian Express*, 20 September 2022.

72 **official directives were issued calling for the inspection of churches**: Nikhila Henry, 'Not Just a "Survey": Karnataka Govt Gets Intelligence Wing to Spy on Churches', *The Quint*, 23 October 2021.

73 **the tahsildar was transferred without a posting**: 'Karnataka Officer Whose Survey Debunked Forced Conversion Claims Gets Transferred', *The News Minute*, 16 December 2021.

74 **a wave of attacks erupted against Christians**: Anusha Ravi Sood, Attacks' on Christian prayer meets continue in Karnataka after anti-conversion bill brought in, *ThePrint*, 4 January, 2022

74 **a ghar wapsi or homecoming ceremony**: 'MLA Goolihatti Shekhar Mother Back to Hinduism', YouTube, 10 October 2021, <www.youtube.com/watch?v=Cczpl1Zi8-Y>.

76 **They destroyed temples, transferred their wealth to Catholic orders**: Ângela Barreto Xavier, *Religion and Empire in Portuguese India: Conversion, Resistance, and the Making of Goa*. New York: SUNY Press, 2022, pp. 70–92.

77 **Christian missions followed in the footsteps of the East India Company**: Chad M. Bauman, *Anti-Christian Violence in India*, New York: Cornell University Press, 2020.

77 **British rule created conditions favourable for Christian missions to proselytize**: John C. B. Webster, *A Social History of Christianity: North-west India Since 1800*, Oxford University Press, 2018.

77 **the story of how Thomas, one of the twelve apostles of Jesus, travelled to India**: Siddhartha Sarma, *Carpenters and Kings: Western Christianity and the Idea of India*, Gurugram: Penguin Random House India Private Limited, 2019.

78 **The early harbingers of the good news**: R. S. Sugirtharajah, *The Bible and Asia: From the Pre-Christian Era to the Postcolonial Age*, Harvard University Press, 2013.

78 **Lower-caste communities were the first to convert**: Xavier, *Religion and Empire in Portuguese India*.

78 **first converts to Christianity in nineteenth-century Delhi were largely from Dalit groups**: Webster, *A Social History of Christianity*.

78 **Adivasis converted to Christianity and felt empowered**: Rowena Robinson, Joseph Marianus Kujur, *Margins of Faith: Dalit and Tribal Christianity in India*, New Delhi: SAGE Publications, 2010.

79 **While a change in religion does not automatically bar Adivasis**: *Kartik Oraon vs David Munzni And Anr*, AIR 1964 Pat 201, 14 November 1963, <https://indiankanoon.org/doc/204475/>.

82 **'We don't change people's religion...'**: Sarbeswar Sahoo, *Pentecostalism and Politics of Conversion in India*, Cambridge: Cambridge University Press, 2018.

83 **The report, authored by the Justice Ranganath Mishra Commission**: Ministry of Law, Justice and Company Affairs, National Commission to Review the Working of the Constitution

(NCRWC) Report, Vol. 1 and 2. Government of India, 2002, <legalaffairs.gov.in/national-commission-   review-working-constitution-ncrwc-report>; Satish Deshpande, 'Dalits in the Muslim and Christian Communities: A Status Report on Current Social Scientific Knowledge', National Commission for Minorities, Government of India, 2008, <ncm.nic.in/ncm/research_studies/dalit_muslim_christian.pdf>; Ministry of Minority Affairs, Report of the National Commission for Religious and Linguistic Minorities, Government of India, 2007, <www.minorityaffairs.gov.in/WriteReadData/ RTF1984/1658830363.pdf>.

83   **But the government told the Supreme Court that the report was 'myopic'**: Satya Prakash, 'Centre rejects 'myopic' Rangnath Misra report that favoured Scheduled Caste status for Dalit converts', *The Tribune*, 7 December 2022.

83   **announced the setting up of a new commission**: Ministry of Social Justice and Empowerment, Notification, Government of India, 6 October 2022, <egazette.gov.in/WriteReadData/2022/239368. pdf>.

83   **Several BJP leaders have echoed this view**: 'Tribals Converting to Other Religions Should Not Get Reservation Benefits: BJP MP Nishikant Dubey', *Outlook*, 14 December 2022; 'Tribals Who Convert Will Be Denied Reservation Benefits: Mansukh Vasava', *Indian Express*, 15 November 2021.

83   **Additionally, the stigma attached to religious conversion**: Sahoo, *Pentecostalism and Politics of Conversion in India*.

84   **They said they had experienced social and economic well-being**: R. S. Shah and T. S. Shah, 'Pentecost Amid Pujas: Charismatic Christianity and Dalit Women in Twenty-First Century India', *Global Pentecostalism in the 21st Century*, P. L. Berger and R. W. Hefner (eds.), Indiana University Press, 2013.

84   **'They believe...that the Spirit can enter ordinary mortals...'**: 'Christianity Reborn', *The Economist*, 19 December 2006.

85   **'In our Hindu religion, there are 33 crore gods...'**: Supriya Sharma, 'As Conversion Debate Rages, Christ Is Part of the Hindu Pantheon in One Madhya Pradesh Village', *Scroll.in*, 13 January 2015.

86   **Christian believers in sixteen villages woke up to copycat attacks**: Chhattisgarh Bachao Andolan, '"Roko, Toko, Thoko" – a Report on the Violence Against the Church-going Adivasi

Community in Bastar, Chhattisgarh', *Groundxero*, 3 January 2023, <www.groundxero.in/2023/01/03/roko-toko-thoko-a-report-on-the-violence-against-the-church%e2%80%90going-adivasi-community-in-bastar-chhattisgarh>.

86   **the Manch held rallies in Bastar through 2022**: 'Janjati Suraksha Manch to Organise Massive Rally in Chhattisgarh to Press for Delisting of Converted Tribals', *Organiser*, 5 May 2022, <organiser.org/2022/05/05/79558/bharat/janjati-suraksha-manch-to-organise-massive-rally-in-chhattisgarh-to-press-for-delisting-of-converted-tribals>.

86   **'They cannot take the benefits of Adivasis…'**: Malini Subramaniam, 'In Bastar, an RSS Campaign Led by a BJP Leader Stoked Violence Against Christian Adivasis', *Scroll.in*, 7 January 2023.

87   **The police followed in their footsteps**: Aishwarya Iyer, 'Investigation: How VHP and Madhya Pradesh Police Colluded to Put a Christian Pastor in Jail', *Scroll.in*, 22 December 2021.

87   **But when a reporter interviewed the priest**: Ibid.

87   **The temple priest told the reporter that the police had summoned him**: Ibid.

87   **assailants chanting Hindu devotional songs inside a Christian prayer hall**: Nehal Kidwai, 'Watch: Right-Wing Activists Sing Bhajans at Karnataka Church as "Protest"'. *NDTV. com*, 18 October 2021.

88   **'What proof do you have of forced conversion?'**: 'Video | Spike in Cases of Violence Against Christians', *NDTV.com*, 1 December 2021.

88   **'over twenty churches were burned or destroyed…'**: 'Politics by Other Means: Attacks Against Christians in India', *Human Rights Watch*, 1 October 1999.

88   **They distributed pamphlets labelling Christian evangelists as devils**: Translated and reproduced in a report by the Citizen's Commission on Persecution of Christians in Gujarat, *Violence in Gujarat: Report of the Citizen's Commission on Persecution of Christians in Gujarat,* National Alliance of Women, 1 April 1999, <cjp.org.in/wp-content/uploads/2020/07/Violence-in-Gujarat-Final_.pdf>.

89   **between 1981-1991, Dangs had seen a four-fold jump in its Christian population**: Parliament Written answer. 23 February 1999, <https://eparlib.nic.in/bitstream/123456789/798385/1/12_IV_23021999_p66_p67_32.

pdf>; 'Religion, Part 4 B (II)', 1991 Census of India, Office of the Registrar General and Census Commissioner of India, Government of India, 1991, <http://lsi.gov.in:8081/jspui/bitstream/123456789/3905/1/37225_1991_ REL.pdf>.

89 **In fact, the allegation of forced conversion was ruled out**: 'Minority Panel Finds Sangh Parivar Forcibly Reconverted Tribals', *Rediff. com*, 8 January 1999, <www.rediff.com/news/1999/jan/08min.htm>; *Violence in Gujarat.*

89 **over 50 people died, scores of women including nuns were raped**: Bauman, *Anti-Christian Violence in India.*

89 **Maoist insurgents took responsibility for the killing:** 'We killed Swami Lakshmanananda: Maoists', *NDTV.com, October 5 2008.*

90 **RSS and BJP went on to project the Odisha violence**: Bauman, *Anti-Christian Violence in India.*

90 **Christians were being forced to convert to Hinduism**: Saumya Uma, *Kandhamal: The Law Must Change Its Course,* Vrinda Grover (ed.), New Delhi: Multiple Action Research Group, 2010.

91 **moved a clause to insert a ban on forced conversions**: Constituent Assembly Debates, Vol. 3. 1 May 1947, <https://eparlib.nic.in/ bitstream/123456789/762959/1/cad_01-05-1947. pdf>.

91 **'...it is admitted that in the law of the land forcible conversion is illegal...'**: Constituent Assembly Debates, Vol. 5. 30 Aug. 1947, <https://eparlib.nic. in/ bitstream/123456789/762981/1/cad_30-08-1947. pdf#search=null%20 1947>.

92 **'In the present context what can this word "propagation"... mean?...'**: Constituent Assembly Debates, Vol. 7. 6 Dec. 1947, <https://eparlib.nic. in/ bitstream/123456789/762992/1/cad_06-12-1948. pdf#search=null%20 1948>.

92 **It failed to muster support**: Lok Sabha Debates, Indian Converts (Regulation and Registration) Bill, Vol. VII, Session no. VIII, 24 Dec. 1954, <https://eparlib.nic.in/ bitstream/123456789/55966/1/lsd_01_08_24-12-1954. pdf>; Lok Sabha Debates, Indian Converts (Regulation and Registration) Bill, 2 December 1955, <https://eparlib.nic.in/ bitstream/123456789/895385/1/01_XI_02- 12-1955_p69_p82_ PII.pdf>.

93   **'the   manifestation   of   understandable   postcolonial anxieties…'**: Chad M Bauman, 'Postcolonial Anxiety and Anti-Conversion Sentiment in the Report of the Christian Missionary Activities Enquiry Committee', *International Journal of Hindu Studies*, 2008, pp. 181–213.

93   **'any attempt by force or fraud or threats or illicit means or grants of financial or other aid…'**: 'Report of the Christian Missionary Activities Enquiry Committee, Madhya Pradesh, 1956, Vol. I', Central Secretariat Library, Government of India, 1956, <indianculture.gov.in/reports-proceedings/report-christian-missionary-activities-enquiry-committee-madhya-pradesh-1956>.

94   **The court defined propagation in strictly dictionary terms**: Rev. Stanislaus vs The State of Madhya Pradesh. 1977 AIR 908, 17 Jan. 1977, https://main.sci.gov.in/jonew/judis/5403.pdf.

94   **'Successful propagation of religion would result in conversion…'**: H. M. Seervai, *Constitutional Law of India: A Critical Commentary*. N. M. Tripathi Pvt. Ltd., 1983, <archive.org/details/constitutionalla0000seer/ page/n5/mode/2up>.

96   **'farcically, if a missionary informs a person…'**: Shoaib Daniyal, 'How India Uses the Absurd Charge of "forced Religious Conversions" to Target Minorities and Dalits', *Scroll.in*, 14 April 2017.

96   **So, a person preaching that 'Adam was the first man on earth'**: Ibid.

97   **'A person not only has a right of conscience…'**: Evangelical Fellowship of India vs. The State of Himachal Pradesh, CWP No. 438 of 2011, 30 August 2012, <https://www.casemine.com/judgement/in/5ac5e4874a93261aa7937710>.

97   **'I will give you names of places, please send your cameras there…'**: 'NDTV Exclusive: Basavaraj Bommai Says BJP Has Given Him "a Free Hand"', *NDTV.com*, interview by Sreenivasan Jain, 27 August 2022.

99   **Even the Supreme Court in 2021 threatened to impose costs on him**: Umang Poddar, 'Petitions Dismissed Thrice, the SC Is Finally Hearing a BJP Leader's Plea on 'Forced' Conversion', *Scroll.in*, 11 December 2022.

99   **centre to file its response on how it plans to 'curb such forced conversion'**: Ashwini Kumar Upadhyay vs Union of India & Ors, WP (Civil) No. 63/2022, 14 November 2022, <https://main.sci.gov.in/

supremecourt/2022/3197/3197_2022_5_48_39663_Order_14-Nov-2022. pdf>.

100 **media reports had punctured holes in the allegations**: Aarefa Johari and Aishwarya Iyer, 'How Hindutva Hijacked India's Child Protection Body', *Scroll.in*, 2 February 2022.

100 **media reported that the children were already Christian**: Prateek Goyal, 'Behind Attack on MP School, Hindutva Outfit's Conversion Claim, NCPCR Letter, and a YouTube Channel', *Newslaundry*, 14 December 2021.

100 **a viral video from October 2021, of a student being beaten**: Mission Ambedkar (@MissionAmbedkar), 'Caste cruelty in schools. Physics teacher of a govt school brutally flogged and kicked a SC minor boy while holding him by his hair. This mind distracting video is from TN's Cuddalore. #CrushTheCaste', X.com, 15 October 2021, <https://twitter.com/MissionAmbedkar/status/1448890965054263299?s=20&t=NDgHhSj SjHyIqhcwUvoN3w>.

100-101 **A factcheck of the video**: 'TN Teacher Who Brutally Thrashed a Class 12 Student Arrested', *The News Minute*, 15 October 2021.

101 **Upadhyay walked away from our cameras**: Sreenivasan Jain and Mariyam Alavi, 'Video | Forced Conversions: Hype Vs Reality', *NDTV.com*, 19 November 2022.

101 **Lavanya Muruganandam, a Class 12 student at Sacred Heart Convent**: Sreedevi Jayarajan, 'TN student Lavanya's death: Cops say conversion angle, video's origin being probed', *The News Minute*, 21 January 2022.

101 **Based on the family's complaint**: FIR in the case related to Lavanya Muruganandam, <https:// cbi.gov.in/assets/files/fir/14907382097b5f5a12-992f-4c2f-bcfb-c1694435c888FIRRC01of2022.PDF>.

101 **a viral video, recorded two days earlier by Muthuvel**: Legal Rights Protection Forum (@lawinforce), Post, 'EXTREMELY SHOCKING: 'They (school) asked my parents in my presence, if they can convert me to Christianity, they would help her for further studies. Since I didn't accept, they kept torturing me. - Statement of a girl who committed suicide (1/n)', X.com, 20 January 2022, <https://twitter.com/lawinforce/status/1483989288782286848?s=20>; JagathKrishna Yadav (@ JagathKrishnaIN), 'Ms. Lavanya, student of St. Mary's High school, Ariyalur Tamil Nadu committed suicide due to the coercive tactics of forced

religious conversion by the school ½', X.com, 21 January 2022, <https:// twitter.com/JagathKrishnaIN/status/148446242260 1572354?s=20>; Laasya Shekhar, 'Lavanya Suicide Case: "Forced Conversion" Vs "Family Abuse", Measured Reportage Vs Trial by Media', *Newslaundry*, 5 February 2022.

104 **a demand also made by the state unit of the Tamil Nadu BJP**: Divya Chandrababu, 'Tamil Nadu girl suicide: BJP seeks CBI probe, Madurai Archbishop denies religious conversion', Hindustan Times, 24 January 2022.

104 **The court agreed**: Special Leave Petition filed by the Director General of Police & Ors in the Supreme Court of India against impugned final judgement and order dated 21.01.2022 in Crl.O.P. (MD) SR No. 3264 of 2022, orders dated 22.01.2022, 24.01.2022 and 31.01.2022 in Crl.O.P. (MD) No. 1344 of 2022 passed by the Madurai Bench of Madras High Court.

CHAPTER 4: MUSLIM APPEASEMENT

108 **Six of every hundred children born in the state die before the age of five**: 'Economic Survey 2022-23', Ministry of Finance, Government of India, 2023, <www.indiabudget.gov. in/economicsurvey/doc/stat/tab814.pdf>; 'Child Mortality Estimates', United Nations Inter-agency Group for Child Mortality Estimation, <https://childmortality.org/>.

108 **'And the rest goes to Muslims.'**: 'PM Modi's Speech at Public Rally in Fatehpur, Uttar Pradesh', YouTube, 19 February, 2017, <www.youtube.com/watch?v=3EYfTG3P1oA>.

108 **a scheme to fortify the boundary walls of Muslim graveyards**: Finance Department, Budget, Grant no. 48, Minorities Welfare Department, Government of Uttar Pradesh, 2012-2017;

109 **the government also sanctioned funds for Hindu cremation grounds:** Finance Department, Budget, Grant no. 14, Agriculture and other related departments (Panchayati Raj), Government of Uttar Pradesh, 2012-2017.

109 **'If there is electricity during Ramzan...'**: 'PM Modi's Speech at Public Rally in Fatehpur, Uttar Pradesh'.

110 **he claimed that under the Samajwadi Party government**: 'Electricity Was Provided on Eid, but Not on Diwali in UP Earlier: Yogi Adityanath', *Indian Express*, 6 May 2019.

111 **more electricity was supplied in Uttar Pradesh on the day**

of Diwali than on Eid: 'Daily Reports', Grid Controller of India, 2013-2022, <pososo.in/reports/ daily-reports>.

111   **power supply across India is higher in summer months**: Kajal Gaur, et al, 'Analysing the Electricity Demand Pattern', 19th National Power Systems Conference (NPSC), December 2016, <www.iitk.ac.in/ npsc/Papers/NPSC2016/1570293957.pdf>.

111   **the Republic's founders were emphatic**: S. Gopal (ed.), 'Letters to the Premiers of Provinces', Dated 15 October 1947, *Selected Works of Jawaharlal Nehru, Second Series*, Vol. 4, Jawaharlal Nehru Memorial Fund, 1986; S. Gopal (ed.), 'Letters to the Premiers of Provinces' Dated 4 October 1948, *Selected Works of Jawaharlal Nehru, Second Series*, Vol. 7, Jawaharlal Nehru Memorial Fund, 1986.

112   **The total allocation on the Muslim graveyard scheme**: Budget, Grant no. 48, Minorities Welfare Department, Finance Department, Government of Uttar Pradesh, 2012-2017; Finance Department, Total budget estimates, Government of Uttar Pradesh, 2012-2017.

112   **the Tamil Nadu government came under criticism:** '50% Subsidy for 'ulemas' to Buy Two-wheelers, Pension Doubled in Tamil Nadu', *Hindu Janajagruti Samiti*, 21 February 2020, <www. hindujagruti.org/ news/124045.html>.

112   **the ₹4,000 per month pension that the state government gives to temple priests:** Shanmughasundaram J., 'Tamil Nadu CM Launches Enhanced Pension Scheme for Priests and Temple Staff ', *Times of India*, 13 January 2022.

112   **in 2023-24, the total expenditure on the ulema pension scheme was ₹5.4 crores:** Finance Department, Budget, Demand no. 09, Backward Classes, Most Backward Classes and Minorities Welfare Department 2023-24, Government of Tamil Nadu, 2023; 'Tamil Nadu Budget Analysis 2023- 24', PRS Legislative Research, 29 March 2023, <prsindia.org/files/budget/ budget_state/tamil-nadu/2023/TN_Budget_Analysis_2023-24.pdf>.

113   **the Prime Minister's Office had to issue a clarification:** 'Press Release: Clarifications on PM's Reference to "First Claim on Resources"', *Former Prime Minister of India: Dr Manmohan Singh*, 10 December 2006, <archivepmo.nic.in/drmanmohansingh/press-details. php?nodeid=516>.

113   **a committee headed by a retired judge Rajinder Sachar:** Prime Minister's High Level Committee, *Social, Economic and Educational Status of the Muslim Community of India*, Government

of India, November 2006, <www.minorityaffairs.gov.in/ WriteReadData/ RTF1984/7830578798.pdf>.

114 **A social media post from January 2023:** Postcard English, 'Musl*ms must have first claim on resources', Facebook, 21 January 2023, <https://www.facebook.com/groups/286465715201744/ permalink/1574102193104750/>.

115 **Sikhs had the highest average monthly expenditure:** National Sample Survey Office, 'Employment and Unemployment Situation Among Major Religious Groups in India', NSS 68th Round, July 2011-June 2012, Report No. 568, Ministry of Statistics and Programme Implementation, February 2016, <www.mospi.gov.in/sites/default/files/   publication_reports/nss_ report_568_19feb16.pdf>.

115 **Illiteracy is the highest among Muslims:** 2011 Census of India, Office of the Registrar General and Census Commissioner of India, Government of India, 2011.

115 **Muslims lag behind on salaried jobs and regular wages:** National Sample Survey Office, Periodic Labour Force Survey (PLFS): Annual Report July 2021-June 2022, Ministry of Statistics and Programme Implementation, February 2023, <www.mospi.gov.in/sites/default/files/publication_reports/ AnnualReportPLFS2021-22F1.pdf>.

115 **only 2.67 per cent of the senior leadership of the top 500 companies:** Naren Karunakaran, 'Muslims Constitute 14% of India, but Just 3% of India Inc', *Economic Times*, 7 September 2015.

116 **Muslim representation in the police force hovered between 3-4 per cent:** 'India Justice Report: Ranking States on Police, Judiciary, Prisons and Legal Aid, Tata Trusts', October 2019, <indiajusticereport.org/files/IJR_2019_ Full_Report.pdf>. (The report does not include data for Jammu and Kashmir.)

117 **budgetary allocations to the Ministry of Minority Affairs:** Ministry of Finance, Demands for Grants, Government of India, 2006-2024.

117 **Welfare measures for Scheduled Castes and Scheduled Tribes:** Paul Divakar, et al, 'How Effective Have NDA's SC/ST Budgets Been? An Analysis of the Last Five Years', *The Wire*, 4 July 2019.

118 **'we find suggestive evidence that the basket of affirmative action policies...':** Sam Asher, et al, 'Intergenerational Mobility in India: New Measures and Estimates Across Time and Social

Groups', September 2022, <paulnovosad. com/pdf/anr-india-mobility.pdf>.

118 **Of every 100 Muslim children, 85 are in school:** National Statistical Office, 'Household Social Consumption on Education in India', NSS 75th Round, July 2017-June 2018, Report no. 585, Ministry of Statistics and Programme Implementation, 2018, <mospi.gov.in/sites/ default/files/publication_reports/ Report_585_75th_round_Education_ final_1507_0.pdf>.

118 **Muslim enrolment numbers have decreased by 8 per cent:** Christophe Jaffrelot and A. Kalaiyarasan, 'Muslims in Higher Education: A Sobering Tale', *Indian Express*, 9 May 2023.

118–19 **only 4.65 per cent of the 41.3 million students enrolled in colleges and universities in 2020–21 were Muslim:** Ministry of Education, All India Survey on Higher Education (AISHE) 2020-21, Government of India, aishe.gov.in/aishe/BlankDCF/ AISHE%20 Final%20Report%202020-21.pdf.

119 **The per capita annual income of Muslims is lower than Dalit Hindus:** Christophe Jaffrelot and A. Kalaiyarasan, 'The Myth of Appeasement', *Indian Express*, 19 April 2018.

119 **India's home minister praised the move:** 'Karnataka Muslim Quota Scrapped: Amit Shah Lauds Bommai Govt, Congress Says Bid to Sow Discord', *Indian Express*, 26 March 2023.

120 **For decades, Hindutva organizations have railed against:** Purnima S. Tripathi, 'Taming of the VHP', *Frontline*, 7 November 2003.

120 **Britain used the hajj to shore up its image in the Muslim world:** John Slight, *The British Empire and the Hajj: 1865–1956*, Harvard University Press, 2015.

120 **The hajj scheme was denounced by Muslims leaders too:** Javed Anand, 'Should the Haj Subsidy Go?', *Sabrang India*, 3 January 2001, <sabrangindia.in/article/should-haj-subsidy-go>.

120 **Air India justified the higher fares:** Shauvik Ghosh, 'Haj Subsidy Has Air India Fuming', *Indian Express*, 12 September 2008.

121 **they said the hajj subsidy was un-Islamic:** Javed, 'Should the Haj Subsidy Go?'.

121 **'In our opinion, if only a relatively small part…':** *Prafull Goradia vs Union of India*, WP (Civil) No. 01 of 2007, 28 January 2011, <https://main.sci.gov.in/jonew/judis/37406.pdf>.

122 **It asked for the hajj subsidy to be phased out:** *Union of India & Ors vs Rafique Shaikh Bhikan & Anr*, SLP (CIVIL)

NO.28609/2011, 30 April 2012, <https://main.sci.gov.in/jonew/judis/39296.pdf>.

122   **the Modi government announced the end of the subsidy:** Kishan G. Reddy, (@kishanreddybjp), Post, 'Modi government's decision to scrap the Haj subsidy will enhance the social structure of the minority community and empower young girls and women as the money will now be used on schools, healthcare and other basic infrastructure for their welfare', X.com, 17 January 2018, <https://twitter.com/kishanreddybjp/status/953508669932552197?s=20&t=2jbEf-fPUEA1BoB0Jy3Y6g>.

122   **₹350 crore per year:** Air India Division. 'Subsidy Given by Government to the Haj Pilgrims Under Government Quota', Ministry of Civil Aviation, 2017, <www. civilaviation.gov.in/sites/default/files/Haj%20Sabsidy%20E%20%281%29. pdf>.

122   **the government budgeted ₹4,236 crore in a single year for the Ardh Kumbh festival:** Rajeev Mani, 'With Budgetary Provision, Major Kumbh Mela Work to Get a Push in Uttar Pradesh', Times of India, 7 December 2022; Prayagraj Mela Authority, 'Making of Kumbh 2019', Maneck E. Davar, <hms. cdoprayagraj. in/download/MakingOfKumbh2019.pdf>.

123   **Several states provide financial assistance to pilgrims travelling to the Kailash Mansarovar lake:** Devasthan Department, Kailash Mansarovar Darshan Yatra, Government of Rajasthan, <devasthan.rajasthan.gov.in/Files/Kalish_Mansrovar_Yatra. pdf>; Department of Religious Affairs, 'About Kailash Mansarovar Yatra', Government of Uttar Pradesh, <http://updharmarthkarya.in/booking/ KM/Home/AboutKailashMansarovarYatra>; Tourism Department, Notification No.TM/AP.I/2016/2620, Government of Haryana, 12 July 2016, <haryanatourism.gov.in/WriteReadData/downloads/e_kailash. pdf>; 'How State Govts Sponsor Pilgrims to Haridwar, Ajmer or Jerusalem', *Indian Express*, 17 January 2018; Tourism Board, Kailash Mansarovar Teerth Yatra, Government of Chhattisgarh, <https://www.chhattisgarhtourism. in/pdf/registration/002.pdf>; Hindu Religious Institutions And Charitable Endowments Department, 'Financial Assistance to Manasa Sarovara Pilgrims', Government of Karnataka, <https://itms.kar.nic.in/ hrcehome/hrce_manasa_sarovara.php>; Directorate of Religious Trust and Endowment. Annual Administrative Report, Government of Madhya Pradesh, 6 June 2006, <https://dharmasva.mp.gov.in/uploads/files/kailsh.

pdf>; Gujarat Pavitra Yatradham Vikas Board, Kailash Mansarovar Yatra, Government of Gujarat, <https://yatradham.gujarat.gov.in/ Documents/ Scheme_2017-5-18_651.pdf>.

123 **the annual expenditure on the scheme rose:** Finance Department, Budget, Demand no. 51, Religious Trusts and Endowments Department 2013-14, Government of Madhya Pradesh, 2013, <https://finance.mp.gov.in/uploads/budget/0617. pdf>; Finance Department, Budget, Demand no. 51, Religious Trusts and Endowments Department 2017-18, Government of Madhya Pradesh, 2017, <https:// finance.mp.gov.in/uploads/ budget/063.pdf>.

123 **Expenditure on the scheme rose to ₹45 crore:** Finance Department, Budget Estimates, Scheme-wise Provision 2017-18, Government of Chhattisgarh, 2017, <finance.cg.gov.in/budget_ doc/2017- 2018/Book/26/S-26.pdf>.

123 **it allocated ₹80 crore for the scheme:** Finance Department, Budget, Demand No. 10, Development, 2023- 24, Government of NCT of Delhi, 2023, <https://finance.delhi.gov.in/ sites/ default/files/Finance/generic_multiple_files/demand_no_10.pdf>; Document shared by an official of the Delhi government in May 2023.

124 **the ministry listed twenty-three sites that had received about ₹18 crore:** 'Unstarred Question no. 3847', *Rajya Sabha Answers*, 6 April 2023.

125 **The Hindu Right asks: why does the government:** Sonia Hinduja (t; egkdky) (@hinduja_sonia), Post, 'Article 30 of Nehru ji allows a Muslim to attend the Quran in the madrasa. Kristin had to read the Bible in the convent school, but in any school, the Hindu cannot read the Gita, Ramayana holy scripture in any school because Section 30A does not allow it. Remove30a', X.com, 21 November 2019, https://twitter.com/hinduja_ sonia/ status/1197480501071630336?s=20; রণবীর ভট্টাচার্য্য (ভেতো বাঙালী) (@BhattacharyaRa7), Post, 'Constitution allows madrasas to teach Quran but Article 30(A) says that Bhagavad Gita cannot be read in schools. Article gives the impression that the Constitution is biased on the teaching of religious text.giving much influence to minority || No support at all', X.com, 17 September 2019, <https://twitter.com/BhattacharyaRa7/status/1173894339262443 520?s=20>.

125 **Ban madrasas, he warned the government:** Imran Khan, (@

KeypadGuerilla), '#pramodmuthalik of #sriramsene has demanded from state and central govt to ban #Madrasas. Muthalik says #Hindu tax payers money is being wasted on madrasa education in the country. Muthalik says that if it is not done. Sri Ram Sene will start an active campaign, #Karnataka', X.com, 15 May, 2022, <https://twitter.com/ KeypadGuerilla/status/1525722272367267 841?s=20>.

126   ₹1,138 crore has been spent on 21,000 madrasas: Ministry of Education, Central Sponsored Scheme for Providing Quality Education in Madrasa (SPQEM), Government of India, <www. education. gov.in/sites/upload_files/mhrd/files/upload_ document/SPQEM-scheme. pdf>; Avinash Kumar Singh, et al., 'Evaluation of the Implementation of the Scheme for Providing Quality Education in Madrasas (SPQEM)', National Institute of Educational Planning and Administration, January 2018, <www. education.gov.in/hi/sites/upload_files/mhrd/files/upload_ document/ spemm_report.pdf>.

126   India's overall school budget in 2018 was ₹50,000 crore: Ministry of Finance, Budget, Demand No. 57, Ministry of Human Resource Development, 2018-19, Government of India, 2018, <www. indiabudget.gov.in/budget2018-2019/ub2018-19/eb/ sbe57.pdf>.

126   the number of teachers supported under the scheme came down: Department-related Parliamentary Standing Committee on Human Resource Development, Demands for Grants 2018-19 (Demand No. 57) of the Department of School Education and Literacy, Rajya Sabha Secretariat, 2018. <164.100.47.5/ committee_web/ReportFile/16/98/305_2018_6_17. pdf>.

126   Bihar's minorities welfare department allocated ₹547 crore for madrasa education: Finance Department, Budget, Demand No. 30, Minority Welfare Department 2023-24, Government of Bihar, 2023; Finance Department, Budget, Demand No. 21, Education Department 2023-23, Government of Bihar, 2023.

126   others ranged between 2.80 per cent for West Bengal: Finance Department, Budget Demand No. 38, Minority Affairs and Madrasah Education 2023-24. Government of West Bengal, 2023; Finance Department, Budget, Demand No. 15, School Education 2023-24, Government of West Bengal, 2023.

126   0.70 per cent for Jharkhand: Finance Department, Budget, Demand No. 44, 58 & 59, School Education & Literacy, Secondary

Education, and Primary Education Departments 2023-24. Government of Jharkhand, 2023.

126 **0.05 per cent for Uttarakhand:** Finance Department, Budget, Grant no. 11, Education, Sports, Youth Welfare and Culture 2023-24, Government of Uttarakhand, 2023; Finance Department, Budget, Grant no. 15, Welfare Schemes 2023-24, Government of Uttarakhand, 2023.

127 **43.52 lakh students were enrolled in 26,928 madrasas:** 'Centre to Develop Portal to Gather Data on Madrassas: Parliament Panel', *NDTV.com*, 12 December 2022.

127 **just 1.64 per cent of the 26.52 crore student enrolment in Indian schools:** 'Unified District Information System for Education Plus (UDISE+)', UDISE+, Department of School Education and Literacy, Government of India, <udiseplus.gov. in/#/home>.

127 **only about 2.3 per cent to 4 per cent of Muslim children attend madrasas:** Prime Minister's High Level Committee, *Social, Economic and Educational Status of the Muslim Community of India*, Government of India, November 2006, <www.minorityaffairs.gov. in/WriteReadData/ RTF1984/7830578798.pdf>.

127 **the government has been surveying madrasas:** Satyendra Sarthak, 'In Uttar Pradesh, unpaid honorariums are pushing families of madrasa teachers into financial woes', *Scroll.in*, 30 January 2022.

127 **government-aided madrasas have been closed down:** Karishma Hasnat, 'All about Assam's new bill that will convert govt-aided madrasas to regular schools', ThePrint, 1 January 2021.

127 **Across India, both BJP and Opposition states have promised:** Ishadrita Lahiri, 'Training Future Pandits to "save Sanatana Dharma" — Inside Rajasthan's Ved Vidyalayas, Boosted by Gehlot Govt', *ThePrint*, 18 April 2023; 'MP will register gurukuls, treat them equivalent to mainstream schools: Shivraj', *Business Standard*, 29 April 2018.

127 **Students passing out of these boards:** Basant Kumar Mohanty, 'Equivalence for Vedic School Certificates', *The Telegraph*, 20 September 2022.

128 **In 2022, the education ministers of Gujarat:** 'Gujarat schools to teach Bhagavad Gita', *The Hindu*, 18 March 2022.

128 **Himachal Pradesh said the Bhagavad Gita would be made a mandatory:** 'After Gujarat, Bhagavad Gita to now be taught in

Himachal Pradesh schools', *India Today*, 5 April 2022.

128   **The Gujarat decision was challenged in court:** 'Gujarat HC Issues Notice to Govt on Introducing Bhagavad Gita in Schools', *The Times of India*, 12 July 2022.

128   **The legal challenge did not stop more BJP-ruled states:** Pathi Venkata Thadagath, 'Karnataka Government Plans to Introduce Bhagavad Gita in Schools From December', *Hindustan Times*, 20 September 2022; Shubhomoy Sikdar, 'Religious texts to be taught in M.P. govt. schools: CM Chouhan', *The Hindu*, 24 January 2023.

128   **'These texts have the capacity to make humans moral and complete...':** Sikdar, 'Religious texts to be taught in M.P. govt. schools: CM Chouhan'.

129   **'There is no surer method of rousing the resentment of the minority...':** Jawaharlal Nehru, 'The Problem of Minorities', *Young India*, Mohandas Karamchand Gandhi (ed.), Vol. 12, 15 May 1930, <archive. org/details/HindSwaraj.YoungIndia.Portal.vol12/page/n171/ mode/2up?q=May%2C+1930>.

129   **The final shape of Articles 29 and 30:** Constituent Assembly Debates, Vol III, 28 April 1947 to 2 May 1947, <https://eparlib. nic.in/bitstream/123456789/762962/1/cad_29-04-1947. pdf>.

129   **'States [shall] protect the existence...':** 'Declaration on the Rights of Persons Belonging to National or Ethnic, Religious and Linguistic Minorities', Office of the High Commissioner for Human Rights, 18 December 1992, <www.ohchr.org/ en/instruments-mechanisms/instruments/declaration-rights-persons-belonging-national-or-ethnic#:~:text=their%20own%20 associations.-,Persons%20belonging%20to%20minorities%20 have%20the%20right%20to%20establish%20and,are%20related%20 by%20national%20or>.

129   **made respect for minority rights one of the 'accession criteria':** 'Minority Rights', *The Princeton Encyclopedia of Self-Determination*, Princeton University, <pesd.princeton.edu/ node/531>; 'Accession Criteria', *European Neighbourhood Policy and Enlargement Negotiations (DG NEAR)*, European Commission, <neighbourhood-enlargement.ec.europa.eu/enlargement- policy/ glossary/accession-criteria_en>.

131   **The court upheld their claim to minority status:** *D. A. V. College Etc vs State Of Punjab & Ors*, AIR 1737 SCR 688, 5 May 1971, <https://main.sci.gov.in/judgment/judis/7149.pdf>.

131 **in 2003, the Supreme Court pronounced a landmark verdict:** *T.M.A. Pai Foundation & Ors. vs State of Karnataka & Ors*, WP (Civil) No. 317 of 1993, 31 October 2002, <https://main.sci. gov.in/jonew/ judis/18737.pdf>.

132 **the Supreme Court ruled in Shah Bano's favour:** Mohd. Ahmed Khan vs Shah Bano Begum And Ors, AIR 945 SCR (3) 844, 23 April 1985, <https://main.sci.gov.in/judgment/judis/9303.pdf>.

132 **A delegation of Muslim women met the prime minister:** Mehru Jaffer, 'These Ignorant, Cruel Forces', *The Citizen*, 5 January 2022.

132 **L. K. Advani popularized the term 'pseudosecularism':** Mark Fineman, 'Profile: Riding the Crest of India's Hindu Revival: Lal Krishna Advani May Gain From His Party's Resurgence to National Prominence', *Los Angeles Times*, 11 June 1991, <www. latimes.com/archives/ la-xpm-1991-06-11-wr-628-story.html>.

132 **'required a clear understanding of who owned what...':** Eleanor Newbigin, *The Hindu Family and the Emergence of Modern India: Law, Citizenship and Community* (Cambridge Studies in Indian History and Society). Cambridge: Cambridge University, pp. 16 and 139, 2013

133 **the first proposal for a code of Hindu family law:** Deepa Das Acevedo, 'Developments in Hindu Law From the Colonial to the Present', *Religion Compass*, Vol. 7, No. 7, Wiley, July 2013, pp. 252–62, <https://doi.org/10.1111/rec3.12052>.

133 **'Muslim women could inherit and hold property...'** Rohit De, 'No, The Uniform Civil Code Was Not Deferred Just for Muslims', *Times of India*, 30 September 2017.

134 **'tyrannous to interfere with the religious practices...':** Speech by B. Pocker. Constituent Assembly Debates, 23 November 1948, <https://www.constitutionofindia.net/debates/23-nov-1948/>.

134 **'But I will confess this...':** Speech by J. Nehru, Lok Sabha Debates, Special Marriage Bill. Vol. IV, Session no. VII, 14 September 1954, <https://eparlib. nic.in/bitstream/123456789/55744/1/lsd_01_07_14-09-1954. pdf#search=null%20Lok%20Sabha%20Debates%20[1952%20TO%20 1959]%2001%201954>.

134 **called out as insincere by Ambedkar:** Sumit Sarkar and Tanika Sarkar (eds.), *Women and Social Reform in Modern India: A Reader*,

Bloomington: Indiana University Press, 2008.

135 **recommended abolishing HUF 'given that it is not congruent...':** Law Commission of India, Consultation Paper on Reform of Family Law, Government of India, 31 August 2018, <cdnbbsr.s3waas.gov.in/ s3ca0daec69b5adc880fb464895726dbdf/ uploads/2022/09/2022092674. pdf>.

135 **a Uniform Civil Code was neither 'necessary, desirable or feasible at this stage':** Law Commission of India, Consultation Paper on Reform of Family Law.

135 **the prime minister himself revived discussions on a Uniform Civil Code:** 'PM Narendra Modi bats for uniform civil code', *Times of India,* 27 June 2023.

136 **BJP had decided to go slow on UCC:** Liz Mathew, 'Road to 2024 | Uniform Civil Code: BJP Is Testing the Waters but May Not Take the Plunge Yet', *Indian Express*, 27 June 2023.

136 **'No Muslim woman wants her husband...':** Poulomi Ghosh, '"No Muslim Woman Wants Her Husband to...",: Himanta Biswa on Uniform Civil Code', *Hindustan Times*, 30 April 2022.

136 **prevalence of polygyny among Muslims was 1.9 per cent:** Rema Nagarajan, 'Multiple wives most common among tribals: NFHS data', *Times of India*, 28 July 2022.

136 **Hindu men have more partners on average than Muslim men:** Banjot Kaur, 'Hindu Men Have Highest Number of Multiple Sexual Partners, Sikhs Second: NFHS-5 Data', *The Wire*, 9 August 2022.

EPILOGUE: POWER, FALSEHOODS, AND CONSEQUENCES

136 **In speech after speech, he repeatedly referred to the 'pink revolution':** 'Shri Narendra Modi Addressing a Massive Gathering in Nawada, Bihar HD', YouTube, 15 May 2014, <www.youtube. com/watch?v=3Idwd2YR_ Jc>; 'Modi's "pink Revolution" Speech in Ghaziabad', YouTube, 4 April 2014, <www.youtube. com/watch?v=Nds_d3jwsa8>; 'Duty on Cotton Export and Subsidy on Mutton Export', YouTube, 23 November 2012, <www. youtube.com/watch?v=woxIJe01IiY>.

138 **'The country has heard of a green revolution...':** Shri Narendra Modi Addressing a Massive Gathering in Nawada, Bihar HD', YouTube, 15 May 2014, <www.youtube.com/ watch?v=3Idwd2YR_ Jc>.

138 **The spectre of cow slaughter is one of the oldest:** Anand

A Yang, 'Sacred Symbol and Sacred Space in Rural India: Community Mobilization in the "Anti-Cow Killing" Riot of 1893', *Comparative Studies in Society and History*, Vol. 22, No. 4, Cambridge UP (CUP), October 1980, pp. 576–96, https://doi. org/10.1017/ s0010417500009555; Akshaya Mukul, *Gita Press and the Making of Hindu India*, HarperCollins India, 2015.

138-39 **his words helped fuel an assault on India's Parliament:** 'The very first attack on Parliament', *The Hindu,* 9 November 2016; Shoaib Daniyal, 'Looking back: The first Parliament attack took place in 1966 – and was carried out by gau rakshaks', *Scroll.in*, 28 August 2016.

139 **demanding a national ban on cow slaughter:** In deference to sensitivities over the cow, India's constitution makers had introduced a directive principle which states: 'The state shall endeavour to prohibit slaughtering and smuggling of cattle, calves and other milch and draught cattle'. In accordance with this, several states passed anti-cow slaughter laws from the 1950s onwards.

139 **he asked the protestors to teach those within the walls of Parliament 'a lesson':** Inder Malhotra 'Holy men stir up riots in Delhi', *The Guardian*, 8 November 2016.

139 **Atal Bihari Vajpayee, a future prime minister of India:** Ramachandra Guha, *India After Gandhi: The History of the World's Largest Democracy*, Picador India, 2008.

139 **Some accounts say a policeman, too, was killed:** 'Fact Check: 1966 Incident of Police Firing on Sadhus Goes Viral With Exaggerated Claims', *India Today*, 6 December 2021.

139 **'The latter was actually doing a service...':** Harish Damodaran, 'In Thrall to the Holy Cow', *Indian Express*, 5 April 2018.

140 **India's meat exports have steadily risen in the past several decades:** 'Video | Truth Vs Hype: Myth of Beef Ban', *NDTV.com*, 21 March 2015.

140 **India prohibits the export of cow meat:** Notification by the Ministry of Commerce and Industry, Government of India, 2011, <https://apeda.gov.in/apedawebsite/DGFT_notificationfile/ Notification_82_31_10_2011.pdf>; Indian Meat Industry – Red Meat Manual, Agricultural and Processed Food Products Export Development Authority, Ministry of Commerce and Industry, Government of India https://apeda.gov.in/apedahindi/

Announcements/RED_MEAT_ MANUAL_.pdf.

140   **the UPA subsidy Modi referred to:** Ministry of Commerce & Industry. Subsidy on Agricultural Goods, Press Information Bureau, Government of India, 26 August 2013, <pib.gov. in/ newsite/PrintRelease.aspx?relid=98656#:~:text=Subsidy%20 on%20 Agricultural%20Goods&text=The%20Government%20 is%20also%20 providing,of%20FOB%20value%20of%20exports>.

140   **BJP-led Maharashtra toughened its cow protection laws:** Zeeshan Shaikh, 'Maharashtra Bans Beef, 5 Years Jail, Rs 10,000 Fine for Possession or Sale', *Indian Express*, 2 March 2015.

140   **buffalo meat exports continued to rise:** Sanya Dhingra, 'India's Beef Exports Rise Under Modi Govt Despite Hindu Vigilante Campaign at Home', *ThePrint*, 26 March 2019.

140   **Mohammed Akhlaq was beaten to death:** Supriya Sharma, 'As meat is turned into a political issue in India, a Muslim ironsmith in Dadri pays the price', *Scroll.in*, 2 October 2015.

140   **One leader described the killing as the work of 'innocent children':** Deepshikha Ghosh, 'On Mob Killing Over Beef Rumours, Ex-BJP Lawmaker's Shocker', *NDTV.com*, 30 September 2015.

140   **'If someone insults our mother (the cow)…':** Liz Mathew, 'If Someone Insults Our Mother, We Would Rather Die Than Tolerate It, Warns BJP's Sakshi Maharaj', *Indian Express*, 6 October 2015.

141   **Too much was being made of an isolated instance:** BJP MP terms Dadri lynching a 'small incident', kicks up row', The Hindu, 13 October 2015.

141   **More details on our methodology:** We catalogued instances of cow-related violence reported in mainstream English news outlets by running multiple online searches using keywords like cow slaughter, cow smuggling, cow lynching, beef india, cattle theft, cow vigilante, and gau rakshak. We filtered the results month-wise for increased accuracy. Relying on media reports to build a dataset is an imperfect exercise. It could be argued that the media was not paying attention to cow-related violence before 2014 and digital record-keeping was less comprehensive since the internet was still evolving. But we found that long before 2014, killings in the name of the cow were still considered shocking enough for the media to take note of them. For instance, a mob attack that led to the killings of seven Dalit men in Haryana in 2002 on suspicion that

they were skinning a cow was widely reported in newspapers.

141 **the houses of two factory owners:** Sarabjit Pandher, 'Cow Slaughter Reports Trigger Violence in Punjab Town', *The Hindu*, 10 June 2012.

141 **from 2014 to May 2023, we counted 136 such cow-related attacks:** From 2009 to 2014 is a five-year period, while 2014 to 2023 is nine years. A better way to compare the two periods would be to average out the number of attacks. The average number of attacks in 2009-2014—the pre- Modi period—worked out to 0.02 instances a month. In the Modi years, that figure rose by 62 times to 1.26 attacks a month.

141 **Of those killed, at least 70 per cent were Muslims:** The share of Muslim casualties could be higher, as in some cases the identities of the victims are not clear.

141 **a mob attack that led to the killings of seven Dalit men in Haryana in 2002:** Deepinder, 'Dalit Lynching: Police Incompetence?' *The Tribune*, 23 October 2002.

142 **'won't give tickets to Muslims':** 'No Muslim Candidates For BJP, Says Karnataka Minister', *NDTV.com*, 30 November 2020.

142 **'Young Muslim men are getting involved with Hindu women':** Mala Das (ed.), 'In election-bound Karnataka, deputy chief minister KS Eshwarappa in trouble over allegedly provocative speech', *NDTV.com*, 12 April 2013.

143 **'Efforts began at Tablighi Jamaat event in Delhi...':** 'BJP's Karnataka MP Calls Delhi's Tablighi Jamaat Event 'corona Jihad',' *ThePrint*, 5 April 2020.

143 **'I appeal to the bank in...':** Zoya Rasul (@zoyarasul), 'WATCH: BJP MLA from UP asking a bank in his constituency to assign a different time for Muslims so that they don't mingle with 'common people'. Asks people to stay away from people of a certain biradari in the interest of their family & nation. Where'll this end?', X.com, 17 April 2020, <https://twitter.com/zoyarasul/status/1251179120026890241>.

143 **he promised to bring a law against 'land jihad':** Ratnadip Chowdhury, '"Will Bring Laws to Stop Love, Land Jihad": Amit Shah at Assam Poll Rally', *NDTV.com*, 26 March 2021.

143 **his government was working against 'fertiliser jihad':** Rokibuz Zaman, 'Why Assam's Farmers Are Furious at Himanta Biswa Sarma's "Fertiliser Jihad" Jibe', *Scroll.in*, 8 June 2023.

Made in the USA
Monee, IL
07 May 2026

4653e377-73cd-47b3-932d-51f4bf127381R01